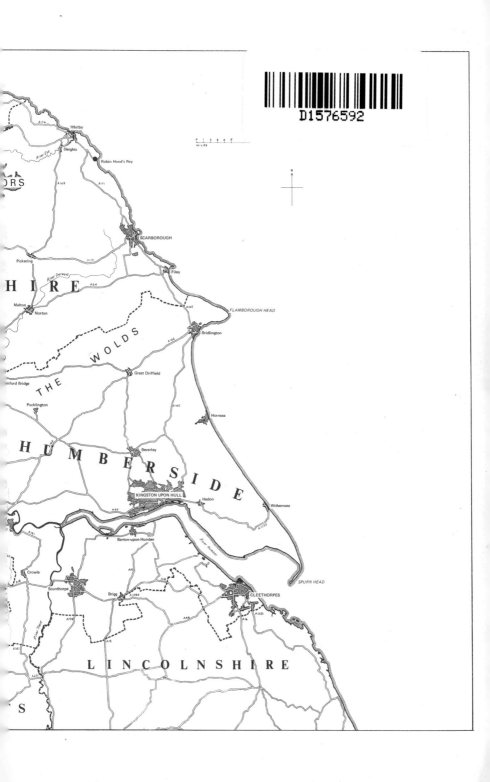

History, People and Places
in
YORKSHIRE

Wensleydale walls, near Hawes.

History, People and Places

in

YORKSHIRE

ARTHUR GAUNT

SPURBOOKS LIMITED

PUBLISHED BY
SPURBOOKS LTD
6 PARADE COURT
BOURNE END
BUCKINGHAMSHIRE

ISBN 0 902875 77 9

MADE AND PRINTED IN GREAT BRITAIN BY
THE GARDEN CITY PRESS LIMITED
LETCHWORTH, HERTFORDSHIRE SG6 1JS

Contents

Dedicated to the memories
of the late Dorothy Turner
and Rowland Turner of Harrogate,
whose interest and encouragement
promoted the writing of this book.

Acknowledgements

The author's thanks are due to Geoffrey N. Wright,
W. R. Mitchell, and Mr. Peter Wigley of Sheffield,
for their help in illustrating this book, and to the
late Dorothy and Rowland Turner, for their
interest and encouragement.

Illustrations

Yorkshire, Past, Present and Future

Any knowledgeable Yorkshire Tyke will tell you that his county has more acres than the number of letters in the Bible. For the record the total acreage is 3,906,940, and somebody who has diligently counted all the letters in the Old and New Testaments puts the number at 3,566,840.

The extent of Yorkshire means that it is the biggest county in the United Kingdom. It is so large that it was long ago divided into 'thirdings' or Ridings, and it has now been divided again under the reorganisation of local government which took effect from April 1974.

The size means that it is blessed with a remarkable variety of scenery, as well as being one of the most important industrial regions in Britain. Even the West Riding overshadowed by factories, has magnets for the tourist, as it replaces its 'dark satanic mills' with new ones and removes the grime from others.

Here and there among the workday places are unusual souvenirs well worth seeking out, old mansions, trading halls of earlier centuries and historic inns.

Whilst it is impossible to divorce the familiar features and associations from a survey of the county's treasures, one purpose of this book is to draw attention to some of the lesser-known objects within the boundaries of Yorkshire. The following pages embrace the delectable and popular Dales, but also include descriptions of numerous other inducements for visits by holidaymakers, tourists, students of the Ridings, and longstanding residents, some of whom are not aware of everything within their county. Like the Londoner who is reputed never to have visited the sights of the capital city, there are Yorkshire natives unacquainted with engaging historic mementoes which they could easily reach.

How was Yorkshire born, geologically? The most distinctive feature, the Pennine Chain, is its backbone. From this divider the

Cautley Crag and the Cross Keys Inn, on the Sedbergh to Kirkby Stephen road.

uplands descend gradually towards the Vale of York and the Vale of Mowbray, though the slopes are intersected by the many dales which lead the Yorkshire rivers eventually to the North Sea.

The western flanks of the Pennines, which surprisingly bring the county to within a dozen miles of the Irish Sea, are steeper and have a character of their own.

The upheavals of primeval time were followed by the Ice Age. Before this ended, about 10,000 years ago, a comparatively recent event geologically, glaciers had scoured out the valleys and left the shape of the county as we know it today. The melting ice created lakes, the remnants of which still exist as Semerwater (North Riding) and Malham Tarn (West Riding), while underground were created the unmatched cave system and the 'potholes' or vertical shafts descending to this subterranean wonderland.

Some of these hidden chambers have provided proof of the occupation of the Pennine region by the earliest humans shortly after the Ice Age.

The Brigantes, the tribe who lived in Yorkshire in pre-Roman times left other marks on the Dales. Traces of the primitive circular huts which they occupied are still discernible in the Fell country.

Howgill Fells, near Sedbergh, within easy reach of the Yorkshire–Cumbria border.

The Anglo-Saxons came to Yorkshire in the fifth century AD, only to suffer attacks by Norse invaders four hundred years later. Their colonisation of North-East England gave us some of the words still used there to the present day.

The Scandinavians remained until William the Conqueror's army landed in Sussex in 1066, and spread northwards.

Evidence of the lives led by these various peoples is not hard to find in Yorkshire. North of Bridlington is the Dane's Dyke, a big entrenchment believed to be a natural cleft which the Danes expanded as a defence for their settlements along the coast. Roman floors, made of coloured tiles to form designs and pictures, have been disclosed at Aldborough, and stones from Roman forts and houses have been built into churches. Hull possesses a stone with an inscription recording that Marcus Ulpius Ianuarius, a kind of sheriff, gave a theatre to Petuaria, the Roman township on the site of the present-day Brough.

Saxon items are preserved in a number of Yorkshire churches. Burnsall Church, Wharfedale, is the custodian of a fine fragment of a Saxon cross covered with interlaced decorations, and in Ilkley churchyard are three Saxon crosses bearing carvings which include figures of the Four Evangelists and evil creatures being trampled upon by Christ.

Norman fonts are fairly common. Bainton, south-west of Driffield, boasts one with a diamond pattern covering the large bowl and a cable moulding round the rim. More striking is the font in North Grimston Church, near Malton. The Normans made it lopsided, and the size, over 3 feet across, is unusual. But the chief appeal is the belief that it is the only font in Britain with a carving of the Descent from the Cross.

The Norman inhabitants of Yorkshire built abbeys, priories, nunneries, and hospitals or almshouses, as well as churches. The baronial families built massive castles. Many of these fortified homes attract tourists today, not only by reason of their grandeur in ruin, but also because they usually have enthralling stories and associations.

The Industrial Revolution of the late eighteenth and early nineteenth centuries was triggered off by the expansion of coal mining, the creation of better roads, and the spreading network of canals and railways. The improved transport system enabled goods such as processed wool and textile fabrics to be more easily distributed.

Pack pony transport went into decline, and cottage spinning and weaving were replaced by steam-driven machinery.

The West Riding, covering 2,775 square miles, is the biggest and richest of the 'thirdings'. The North Riding comes second, with 2,128 square miles, and the East Riding is the smallest, extending over 1,172 square miles.

About 3,500,000 people live in the West Riding, compared with 470,000 or so in the North Riding and approximately 750,000 in the East Riding. But the figures are in a state of flux as a result of changes in industries.

The trend continues, and one outcome during the next few years will probably be an increase in the population of the East Riding. The region already has Britain's third largest seaport at Hull, and the Humber Bridge is confidently expected to expand trade and bring many more workers and their families to the area during the next few years.

More traffic across the Pennines is being encouraged by the M62, the new highway running across England's backbone.

The M62 is in fact a unique road. There are important ones going to a greater height in other parts of the world, but they are closed

Snape Castle, south of Bedale.

when winter arrives. The cross-Pennine motorway has been designed and built for use by heavy traffic every day of the year.

Before the route was selected, scientists made prolonged studies of the way in which weather conditions varied along several possible routes. Meteorological records of the rainfall, snowfall, and wind velocities throughout the years were prepared and considered in connection with the proposed new motorway.

Various ways of overcoming bad weather hazards were investigated by practical tests. The effects of the slope of the highway in increasing or decreasing the amount of snow blown on to it were measured.

Other studies included the trapping of falling snow by trees, and methods of minimising the dangers of gales by enabling vehicles to avoid the sudden onslaught of high winds.

Yorkshire has undergone further changes in recent years as a result of forestry operations. Wide acres have been replanted to make up for the large number of trees felled for industrial and war purposes, while private landowners have been encouraged to follow a tree-planting programme.

Nevertheless, replanting has not restored the landscape to its former appearance. The ancient oaks and other hardwoods have been replaced with conifers. In the eyes of many people this alteration has not been an improvement.

Nowadays the Forestry Commission encourages public interest in the woodlands, placing fewer restrictions upon walkers wishing to traverse them. This facility again is not exactly new. As long ago as the early nineteenth century the incumbent of Bolton Priory Church arranged about thirty miles of walks for the enjoyment of visitors from Yorkshire's industrial districts.

The busy scenes created by motorists around the Priory today are a repetition of the time when crowds arrived by train at the nearby station on the Ilkley–Skipton line or came in horsedrawn wagonettes.

This, then, is a short survey of some of Yorkshire's attractions. The county has many Meccas for anybody able and willing to get around its millions of acres. The description of such spots in the ensuing pages is not intended to be comprehensive or exhaustive, but primarily an introduction to some examples which may be easily found.

But the face of Yorkshire is changing. Industrial predominance is undergoing revision at an increasing speed, and the idea, held outside the county and not by Tykes, that the region is covered by dark satanic mills is being dispelled, and from 1974 new names for old places will be in public use.

The scars of factories which besmirched the cities and towns have already been erased, and the encroachment of Mammon into the county's countryside is being progressively stemmed.

In this revolution a big part is being performed by bodies which have the provision of facilities for leisure pursuits as their major aim. They include Forestry Commission, organisations for reviving defunct railway routes as pleasure lines, and the creation of 'ways' or footpath routes for long-distance walkers.

An example of one method whereby the landscape has been changed can be found by scanning Wharfedale from the highest point of the Skipton–Barden road. The panorama from that viewpoint is dominated by many square miles of thickly growing woodlands. True, the trees are coniferous ones, and not the oaks and other species generally regarded as native to Northern England, but it is not difficult to imagine the far less attractive picture of the same fells in a bare condition.

Aspects of that sort have also been developed around Dalby, Cropton, Doncaster, and in the Cleveland Hills. Altogether the Forest Conservancy has well over 250,000 acres under its wing in Yorkshire, and by far the biggest proportion are under plantation. New forests, or the extensions of existing ones, have been provided in the Langdale, Scawton, Wykeham, Osmotherly, Ampleforth, Jervaulx, Selby, Knaresborough, and Cawthorne regions.

A most significant innovation in recent years has been a big alteration in the policy of the Forestry Commission towards the general public. Not so long ago little encouragement was given to those wishing to use the forest paths, lest fires or other damage was caused by careless visitors.

A much more enlightened attitude has since been adopted, forest walks being opened, with route plans pointing out what to look for. Leaflets indicate where markers have been placed, and give information of interest to walkers.

The Pennine Way, opened after years of agitation for freedom to walk along England's backbone, runs mainly through Yorkshire and has since been augmented by other long-distance footpaths,

The Cleveland Hills.

Mount Grace Priory, North Yorkshire.

notably along the East Riding Wolds and westward in the Wharfedale area.

These 'ways' are not to be envisaged as ribbons of concrete running across the landscape. They are trodden paths, and the 'ways' are created by linking various stretches of that sort by obtaining access to intermediate sections privately owned.

Other outdoor enthusiasts have been responsible for re-opening closed railway services. The first line in Yorkshire to be revived, the Keighley and Worth Valley Railway, was barred to passenger trains after nearly one hundred years' use. Steps to get it operating again were first mooted at a public meeting in Keighley in March 1962, and enthusiasts raised the money needed to take over the line from British Rail.

The line was re-opened on 29th June 1968, and it has since become one of the busiest scenic routes in the country, giving young passengers in particular a thrilling ride as well as carrying adults to the Brontë village of Haworth.

The conversion of defunct lines into roadways has been investigated. An example is the former railway route between Otley

North Yorkshire Moors, Saltergate Inn.

and Burley-in-Wharfedale, considered as providing a much needed bypass round the former cramped town.

An unexpected sidelight on the disappearance of old buildings from our cities and towns is the realisation that in consequence many invaluable reminders of the Industrial Revolution are likely to be lost for ever, unless efforts are made to preserve them. The situation has led to a new branch of study, industrial archaeology, an aspect of our national life comparatively neglected by antiquarians until recently.

The abandoning of canals has given historical importance to locks, bridges, wharves, and barge builders' yards, and the provision of more suitable roads has entailed the demolition of many old toll-houses, making the surviving ones more worth safeguarding as reminders of eighteenth and ninteenth century road transport.

Forges, furnaces, and rolling mills merit attention from this standpoint, and still another aspect of the subject is the preservation of handloom workers' cottages which have not yet been swept away.

An industrial revolution survey has been functioning to deal with the problem, finding out what is worth safeguarding and how it can be carried out. The investigations have been undertaken partly

Typical moorland scene, Dentdale.

by volunteers from universities, technical colleges, schools, museums, learned societies, and national and local authorities.

Some enlightened cities and manufacturing towns have supported industrial archaeology for a number of years. Halifax has brought together a noteworthy collection of the larger type of industrial bygones, and has not restricted the exhibits to objects suitable only for museum cabinets or interior displays. Thus, outside Shibden Hall is an old horse ginny, a large horizonal drum used at one period to raise coal from a local mine.

Now, however, large scale industrial museums are being developed in a surprisingly big way in Yorkshire. An old mill at Armley, Leeds, is being used in this way for the preservation and exhibition of old machinery. A similar venture at Eccleshill, Bradford, attracted 2,000 visitors during its first ten days of opening, though it was far from complete and is still undergoing expansion.

When all its three floors are open it will include textile machinery driven by a big 100 h.p. horizontal steam engine and a variety of looms on which local schoolchildren can try their hand. The atmosphere of bygone millmasters' and mill employees' lives will be conjured up by incandescent gas lighting, horsehair-stuffed

Goathland Village, in Eskdale.

furniture, and a magnificent wooden bath with a shuttered shower from a Victorian home.

Private benefactors are adding to Yorkshire's heritage of souvenirs by establishing museums of their own. Mr. G. W. Shaw, of Richmond, in the North Riding, has created a collection of horse-drawn transport claimed to be the biggest private one in the country. Housed in a former corn mill near Aysgarth Falls, it embraces fine examples of the coachbuilders' craft, many of the vehicles being attractively decorated.

From an original eight exhibits the total number has risen to about a hundred, and some sixty are on show to the public during the summer months. Landaus, coaches, broughams, whiskeys, floats, brakes, wagonettes, barouches, and farm vehicles of all descriptions have been brought together.

A survey of Yorkshire reveals that the county enshrines a vast number of interests and attractions, both public and private to thrill present and future generations. The conservation of these treasures, for the enjoyment of our descendants, is an important duty in this period of change, and the various bodies concerned with preservation merit strong support. The very least that the rest of us can do is to care for the unique heritage of old Yorkshire, as the new counties arise on the fabric of the past.

CHAPTER 1

The Calder Valley

There are more than one hundred dales in Yorkshire. It is, however, hard to say exactly what constitutes a 'dale'.

Are we to apply the term to valleys of any length, or to exclude those which stretch only a short distance? Usually, the Bain, rising between Askrigg Common and Abbotside Common, is looked upon as the shortest river in the county for the length, as it reaches Bainbridge, is a mere two-and-a-half miles.

Again there are rivers which change their name *en route*. A classic instance is in Uredale. Between Wensley, near Middleham, and Aysgarth it is referred to as Wensleydale. Should we count this part as a separate Dale or include it in Uredale?

The longest Yorkshire river, and therefore the longest Dale, is the Swale. In its narrow winding route it traverses eighty-three miles of the North Riding. Second river in the county is the Aire, with its source something of a mystery near Malham. It flows eighty-one miles before emptying into the Ouse near Airmyn. Other important Yorkshire dales in order of length are Wharfedale, the Don Valley, the Derwent Valley, Nidderdale, Calderdale, and the diminutive Esk Valley.

The last-named counterbalances its meagre length of twenty-four miles by presenting enchanting scenery between the hills of Cleveland and the port of Whitby.

The Calder is an industrial river, but not exclusively so. Rising near Burnley it soon switches its loyalty from Lancashire to Yorkshire, passing through or near a variety of interesting places—Heptonstall, Hebden Bridge, Mytholmroyd, Luddenden, Halifax, Hartshead, Wakefield, and Altofts—before joining the Aire at Castleford.

The most westerly part of this dale has such scenic attraction that a number of plans to create a big reservoir by flooding it have

Wainstones, in the Cleveland Hills.

been strongly opposed by ramblers' organisations and other bodies concerned with safeguarding our rural heritage.

Since 1950 the National Trust has been responsible for preserving the woodland on the north bank of Hebden Water, a tributary of the Calder within easy walking distance of Hebden Bridge. This pleasant area of forest was given to the Trust by Lord Savile. A further area of woods and farms, between the stepping stones opposite Hardcastle Crags and the open moorland above the valley, came under the wing of the Trust in the same year as a result of a bequest.

Heptonstall, high above Hebden Bridge, is one of the most alluring Pennine villages. Its wealth of historic relics should give it precedence over many other places renowned as attractive to tourists.

John Wesley found Heptonstall a challenge to his preaching abilities, and he took a keen interest in the inhabitants' efforts to establish a Methodist chapel there.

The founder of Methodism came to Heptonstall many times, and originally the services were held in a seventeenth century farmstead. This building, the home of a widow who sold old clothes and treacle toffee in Wesley's day, was leased to the local Methodists by her. It is still known by its original name of the preaching house.

The crowning achievement of the early Heptonstall Methodists was the erection of a hexagonal chapel in Northgate. 'Crowning' is an apt description, for with Wesley's aid they managed to have a roof put over the singularly shaped place of worship. Local carpenters felt incapable of making such a roof, but when John Wesley heard of their dilemma he instituted enquiries farther afield, and a Rotherham expert agreed to tackle the job.

The most important point about the chapel is that it continues in use today. It is the oldest Methodist chapel in the world and has been used for worship since it was opened more than two hundred years ago.

Heptonstall is also one of the villages claiming distinction because it has two churches in one churchyard. This state of affairs is not as rare as often assumed, but this West Riding example is worth noting. The older church here was founded in the thirteenth century, and was gradually increased in size to accommodate more and more people, until in the early years of the nineteenth century further expansion was halted and a new church was built within the same enclosure.

Today the open shell of the old church engenders an eerie feeling, and the surrounding graveyard has sinister overtones, for it contains the body of a notorious eighteenth century criminal, David Hartley, a leading member of a counterfeiting gang who established an illicit mint in the Cragg Vale area. 'King David' was caught, convicted of murder, and hanged at York in 1770. His remains were eventually sent to Heptonstall for burial. The entry in the church register concerning his burial is written in Latin, although at the date concerned it was already customary to enter such details in English. One treasure in the new Heptonstall Church is the eleven-sided font from the old place of worship.

The hilltop village became more townlike as decades went by. It prospered with the expansion of the wool trade, but the parish registers reveal a distressing time in 1631. Not a single marriage was recorded in that year, yet the number of deaths reached an unprecedented figure. Entire families, including that of the parson, perished from a visitation of the plague. Other records of that grim year describe how grass grew in the streets, and how the scene was one of neglect and decay.

Heptonstall existed long before Hebden Bridge came into being as an industrial centre in the valley below. The township indeed derives its name from the skyscraper village. The title is a corruption of Hepton Brig, and refers to the bridge spanning the Calder which travellers had to cross before starting the stiff climb to Heptonstall.

Luddenden Foot and Mytholmroyd on the way to Sowerby Bridge are irrevocably associated with the Cragg Vale coiners. The road leads to bleak moorlands on the southern fringe of Calderdale, and the gang had their hideout in a remote farmstead which could not be easily approached by unseen strangers.

The essence of the counterfeiters' scheme was their discovery that gold coins of the realm became lighter after being in circulation for some time. So the legally required weight for used sovereigns and guineas was less than that of new ones.

From this circumstance came the idea of filing gold from new gold coins to bring them down to the weight of well-worn ones, and then sell the filings to bullion dealers. It was only a stage further to clip the coins instead of just filing them, and finally to mint guineas with the precious metal.

The Exchequer became disturbed by the threat to the national

Heptonstall—view from Weavers' Square.

monetary system, and the menace to commerce affected West Riding merchants to such a degree that they hired private detectives to trace the source of the counterfeit money.

The repercussions of these illicit activities extended abroad too. In fact the first indication of a big clipping conspiracy in England came to the British Government from Hamburg, where a Halifax man was prosecuted for clipping German coins. His arrest was followed by investigations into the probability that he had offended similarly in Yorkshire.

The trail led to Calderdale and the Cragg Vale farm, but the coiners could not be taken by surprise even at night. They had fierce dogs to give warning of anyone approaching stealthily.

The confederates included David ('King') Hartley's brother-in-law, Thomas Spencer of New House, on the outskirts of Mytholmroyd. The dwelling now belies its name, the walls having defied the storms for more than two centuries.

The home of Isaac Hartley, David's brother, who was also in the gang, stood on the site of another Mytholmroyd house known as Elphaborough Hall. The tightly-knit little township still has its Dusty Miller inn, now a respectable hostelry but a more sinister place two centuries ago.

In 1768 the Government decided to deal with the counterfeiters, and an Excise Officer named Deighton was sent to gather evidence against members of the gang. As a result of his enquiries 'King David' was arrested and imprisoned at York to await trial, and other accomplices were apprehended soon afterwards.

That was in October 1769, but before the detained men could be tried in court members of the gang met at the Dusty Miller to discuss means of helping the imprisoned crooks. The outcome was a plot to slay Deighton, for without his evidence it seemed unlikely that the prisoners at York could be convicted.

Thomas Spencer and Isaac Hartley sought out an assassin willing to murder the Excise man and that loyal but unfortunate Government official was shot dead.

So far from freeing any of the conspirators, the murder prompted still more searching enquiries into their operations, and warrants were issued for the arrest of more men implicated in coin clipping. Some fled from the Mytholmroyd neighbourhood, while those who remained were terrorised by the Hartley and Spencer families into making false statements about the gang.

David Hartley was eventually convicted as a counterfeiter. Isaac Hartley and Thomas Spencer were found guilty of complicity in Deighton's murder. The penalty in each case was death by hanging. 'King' David's remains were left on the public scaffold at York for a time as a grim warning, but his relatives were later allowed as already described to have his body interred in Heptonstall churchyard.

The coin dies from Cragg Vale farmhouse bear the design of Portuguese 4,000-reis gold pieces and are now kept at the Bankfield Museum, Halifax.

The same repository also contains a model of the Halifax Gibbet, designed like a French guillotine, and the actual blade of this gruesome machine of execution also survives. Beheading was the penalty for comparatively petty crimes in the town, such as stealing cloth or wool. Little wonder that in those days a common plea was 'From Hull, Hell and Halifax the Good Lord deliver us'.

A more pleasant possession of the town today is the slender column, terminating like an Oriental minaret, which looks down into the Calder valley from an escarpment near the out-district of King Cross. Wainhouse's Folly, as the structure is often called, is over 200 feet high and takes its name from John Edward Wainhouse, a member of a local family with a long ancestry.

Henry Edwards a local landowner owned dyeworks a quarter of a mile below the spot now occupied by the tower, and conduits to carry away the smoke from the dyehouse were envisaged. Wainhouse's Tower was originally meant to provide an outlet for the fumes, at a point high enough to avoid causing a nuisance.

In point of fact, the structure, far less ornate than it is now, has never emitted smoke. Wainhouse leased his dyeworks to another businessman, who did not need a chimney so remote from the premises. Consequently the flue was never completed, and it was this circumstance, not a feud with Colonel Edwards, which prompted John Edward Wainhouse to turn the hollow column into an observation tower.

It was completed for use in September 1875, after four years of difficult labour. The material came from some nearby quarries owned by Wainhouse, and the structure cost him approximately £10,000 on wages and other expenses.

After his death in 1883 the 'Octagon Tower', as it is more officially called, had a succession of owners. Then in 1918 a Shilling

Subscription Fund was organised, enabling Halifax Corporation to buy and preserve the singular landmark. It incorporates a spiral stairway to the observation galleries, and it is open to the public from time to time.

This odd-looking chimneystack also has a place in radio history. In 1929 it was used as the transmission point for broadcasts from a local radio station. The transmitter had a range of several miles, and the station claimed to have a greater number of listeners than any other radio broadcasting centre in the country.

North-east of Halifax lies the village of Shelf, now part of Bradford. Indistinguished architecturally it has a place in the relatively recent history of the industrial West Riding. Here, as in other parts of the region, it is the custom for the local mills to observe 'tides' or 'wakes', when the factories are shut for a holiday period each August and an exodus takes the workpeople to favourite resorts.

It was this ritual which focused national interest on to Shelf in 1875, when one of its sons, John Hobson Jagger, succeeded in 'breaking the bank at Monte Carlo'. The description relates to such successful gaming that the Casino owners find it necessary to dip into their reserves in order to pay the winner.

J. H. Jagger caused them to do just that, and for a period the authorities feared that a situation which they dreaded, the arrival of a gambler who had found a sure system for winning at the roulette tables, had actually occurred.

An engineer by trade, Jagger customarily saved hard during most of the year and spent these savings on a tiptop holiday each summer. In July 1875 Jagger made his way to London when the factory which employed him closed for the annual 'tide', and from the Metropolis he headed for Monte Carlo.

He did not go there intending to risk his hard-earned savings at the Casino tables, but went primarily to enjoy the glittering scene. But while strolling round the splendidly appointed rooms his interest in engineering prompted him to scrutinise the roulette wheels closely. His practised eyes told him that the cylinders were not up to the standard of workmanship he had expected.

Reflecting on this discovery he concluded that some numbers must inevitably turn up as winners more often than others. To test the theory he engaged a team of clerks to write down the numbers appearing most often at each table. Sure enough, when he tabulated the mass of figures his belief was borne out. The data enabled him to evolve a system which could be relied upon to give better than the usual odds.

Jagger's first night's gambling netted him several hundred pounds. On the second night he was so successful that the other tables were deserted, as holidaymakers from all over the world crowded round to watch the 'Lucky Englishman' pile up still more winnings.

The Casino owners at first suspected a trick, or some collusion between Jagger and the croupier. These suspicions were unfounded, so the authorities concluded (rightly) that the cylinders were somehow involved. Though uncertain of his method, the Casino operators interchanged the cylinders from one table to another, but Jagger's bonanza continued!

He had secretly marked the cylinder which related to his system, so that all he had to do was to look for this cylinder and seat himself at the same table.

Eventually the authorities realised that the crudeness of the cylinders in some way came into his activities, and new ones of better workmanship were substituted.

But by that time Jagger had 'broken the bank' and collected winnings worth about £200,000 by today's standard. He resisted the temptation to continue gambling after realising that his method of winning had become known, returned to his native village and invested his money in property.

His grave is in the churchyard at Shelf and is marked by a tapering column. The inscription recording his death makes no mention of his feat at Monte Carlo. It simply quotes the date when he died. His most lasting memorial is the song which his 'breaking of the bank' is thought to have inspired.

Yorkshire lays serious claim to another and much better known figure—none other than Robin Hood. In recent years the county has stolen some of the lure from Sherwood Forest and its connections with the stories of the famous outlaw and his merry men.

Did they ever exist or are they just folklore characters? An unequivocal answer to the question has yet to be given, but historians and students of folk tales put forward some evidence that Robin was a Yorkshireman, and that many of his escapades took place in the county.

Numerous placenames in Yorkshire suggest that he was accepted

well north of the Tweed in addition to south of it. Robin Hood's
Bay on the north-east coast is an example, though there is no proof
that he practised archery there. Richmond Castle in the North
Riding incorporates a tower named after him, and it is said that
he had ships in readiness at the coastal point just mentioned to put
out to sea if he was in danger on land.

Two wells in Yorkshire, one near Doncaster and the other close
to Fountains Abbey, bear the outlaw's name, and Whitby Abbey
is reputed to have been the setting for an archery demonstration by
Robin and Little John.

Further reminders of Robin and his band include a long-bow
traditionally regarded as once the property of Little John. This
weapon is now in Cannon Hall at Cawthorne, near Barnsley.
Numerous inns perpetuate Robin in their name, the signboard of
such a tavern at Cragg Vale carrying the verse:

> Ye bowmen and ye archers good,
> Come in and drink with Robin Hood.
> If Robin Hood is not at home,
> Come take a glass with Little John.

A still stronger association between Calderdale and Robin Hood's
life and death is to be found at Kirklees, near Brighouse. On the
fringe of a private estate here is to be seen the substantial remains
of a nunnery gatehouse where, according to legend, he retreated
when at last he became old and infirm.

The prioress is said to have been his aunt, but blood-letting, a
common remedy for illness in those days, made him weaker.
Indeed, some students of his life-story believe that the prioress,
ashamed to be related to the bold outlaw, deliberately allowed him
to bleed to death.

Nevertheless he summoned enough strength to blow a blast on
a horn to attract Little John. Arriving at the bedside and suspecting
the prioress's treachery, Robin's henchman wanted to raze the
nunnery, but the ailing leader would not agree. Instead, he asked
for a bow and arrow and made a long-distance shot from the
gatehouse window, commending that he should be buried where
the arrow landed.

Sure enough a gravestone in a railed enclosure on a knoll within
sight of the gatehouse bears an inscription stating that Robin Hood,
Earl of Huntingdon, lies there. The epitaph, in verse, has been the

subject of much controversy, and its authenticity has been seriously questioned.

Investigators have pointed out that the style of lettering concerned was not prevalent in the period when the outlaw is alleged to have robbed the rich and helped the poor. Other students of the tradition, however, have a ready reply to this criticism. They state that the present inscription is a copy of an older one.

Ralph Thoresby, the eminent Leeds historian and antiquary, left a note stating that the verse was copied by Dr. Gale, Dean of York, towards the end of the seventeenth century, and that the existing inscription was carved after the original lettering had been destroyed by souvenir hunters. It is also known that navvies working on the nearby railroad last century added to the destruction of the gravestone by chipping pieces from it and sucking them as a believed cure for toothache!

The earliest known written reference to an outlaw called Robin Hood occurs in a national legal roll or document prepared in 1230, when 32s. 6d. was paid for the belongings of such a fugitive. 'Piers the Plowman', by the fourteenth century poet William Langland, also mentions a heroic figure called Robyn Hood. A significant point, as far as Yorkshire associations with him are concerned, is that the record made in the year 1230 occurs in a section probably dealing with the West Riding.

On the Kirklees gravestone the death of Robin is quoted as 24th December 1247. There is thus a good deal of substantial evidence that his life and death was as closely concerned with Yorkshire as with Nottinghamshire. His name and deeds were handed down in successive centuries as folklore, though there may be some confusion today with the 'Roberdsmen' whose lawlessness resulted in enactments against them as long ago as the reign of Edward I.

"Green Men', or outlaws infesting the forests which used to cover most of England, were mentioned by many authors and poets of bygone periods. Shakespeare refers to a Robin Hood in three of his plays, while lesser writers brought him into the plays and pageants of Tudor and later days.

One of Yorkshire's public reminders of this particular outlaw is again near Kirklees. A tapering unadorned column known as Dumb Steeple is pointed out as having served as a meeting-point for Robin Hood and his band. Luddite rioters used the same pillar as a

Nunnery Gatehouse, Kirklees, near Brighouse. Robin Hood is said to have died here.

marshalling spot before setting out to attack West Riding mills in the early days of the Industrial Revolution.

Also connected with that period is Liversedge parish church, a unique building. It is a monument to the sacrifices made by its first vicar, the Rev. Hammond Roberson, a native of Cawston, Norfolk, who came to Yorkshire after distinguishing himself at Magdalene College, Cambridge.

Coming to Dewsbury in 1779 he offered his services as a private tutor and also founded a private school there, to eke out his small stipend as curate to the Vicar of Dewsbury.

A further achievement of this in-comer from the south-east of England was to establish Sunday schools in the area, similar to those begun by Robert Railes at Gloucester in 1780. Roberson rented out cottages in the town for a shilling a time, and gave religious instruction there to young people.

He fostered secular learning too, and his private school at Dewsbury Moor became so popular that larger premises soon became essential. To meet this demand he moved the pupils to Healds Hall, Liversedge, where the school continued to thrive, amassing him a considerable fortune.

This success enabled him to carry out a big ambition which had long exercised his mind—to build a church of his own. When he saw that Liversedge needed one he offered to erect a place of worship entirely at his own expense. The present Liversedge parish church was ready for use in 1816, but the cost, over £7,000, put the Rev. Roberson into such financial difficulties that he had insufficient money left to provide himself with a vicarage, until wellwishers subscribed to overcome the problem.

A portrait of this remarkable clergyman hangs in the church and conveys a feeling of his sterling character. An active opponent of blood sports, he aroused the enmity of their West Riding supporters by preaching strongly against them.

He also enraged the Luddites who destroyed the machinery then being installed in mills, because they feared that their livelihood as hand-spinners and handloom operatives would be jeopardised. Roberson disapproved of their violence so vehemently that they threatened him with injury unless he altered his attitude towards them.

A secret passage, now sealed, could formerly be entered from the church crypt. The tunnel is believed to have served as an escape route to Healds Hall, enabling the parson and his family to flee to safety if ever the church and vicarage were surrounded by hostile Luddites.

The Rev. Hammond Roberson held strong opinions about the appearance of the churchyard too, and his strict rules about burials continued to be enforced by later incumbents. He insisted that there were to be no interments within 4 feet of the church walls, and he required that the headstones marking the graves were to be uniform and without ornamentation. When the rule about adornments was violated, he had the offending slab uprooted and thrown aside.

He appears in Charlotte Brontë's *Shirley* as the Reverend Matthewson Helstone. He was in fact a personal acquaintance and friend of the Rev. Patrick Brontë, and while Charlotte was a scholar at Roe Head School, near Mirfield, she learned about the Luddites at first hand.

She heard how the rioters met at Dumb Steeple to receive their orders, and she was told how the Liversedge cleric mustered his whole household, providing them with weapons to repel any assault on his church.

This fiery, autocratic, and somewhat eccentric parson was, indeed, a man of many parts. Among his secular accomplishments was the ability to break-in the unmanageable horses of his parishioners.

Dewsbury, today's busy centre producing fancy tweeds and fine worsted fabrics, has retained a Christmas custom founded hundreds of years ago. Every Christmas Eve the tenor bell in the parish church tower is tolled once for every year since the birth of Christ. The practice is known as the Devil's Knell, and the tolling is so arranged that the final stroke coincides with midnight.

There are several accounts of the origin of the rite, one belief being that it is just a perpetuation of the old idea that Satan dare not approach a place where a church bell is pealing. Tolling his knell on Christmas Eve was regarded as a means of keeping the Evil One at bay throughout the next twelve months.

A second explanation is that the Dewsbury bell ritual symbolises Christ's triumph over evil, though critics of this idea are quick to point out that joyful peals would be more appropriate than doleful ringings.

More romantic is the story that the Devil's Knell began when a local nobleman, Thomas de Soothill, sought to atone for murdering a servant boy and throwing his body into a stream. The contrite overlord presented a bell to Dewsbury parish church and instructed that it was to be rung in the way described.

Nowadays, as nearly two thousand strokes have to be rung, the tolling starts well in advance of twelve o'clock. The custom is complicated because a midnight service is held in the church, and tolling has to be suspended during that period. It is then resumed and timed to finish on the stroke of midnight.

Wakefield's historic treasures include the remarkable old bridge spanning the Calder on the southern edge of the town; remarkable not only by reason of its antiquity and the survival of its medieval chantry or chapel, but also because it has survived at all.

The structure was long a hindrance to road traffic, and was under continual threat of demolition or widening which would have ruined its character. Fortunately a different attitude finally prevailed. Instead of being razed or widened, the ancient bridge was allowed to remain and a modern one was erected a few yards upstream.

The chapel, however, has undergone some changes and put to uses which its builders never envisaged. It is said to have been erected in memory of Richard, Duke of York, who was slain at the Battle of Wakefield in 1460. The battle was not fought at this

The chapel on Wakefield Bridge.

river crossing, but near Sandal Magna, on the road to Barnsley, and a pillar there marks the spot where the Duke fell.

The most striking feature of the chantry is the elaborately carved façade, today thoroughly cleaned to reveal its loveliness. But the frontage seen nowadays is not the original. That ancient relic had deteriorated so much by the early years of the nineteenth century that Sir Gilbert Scott was commissioned to restore it in 1847. He gave it a new west front and the old one was transferred to the Kettlethorpe estate, where it still survives as part of a boathouse.

Sir Gilbert Scott's restoration work also weathered seriously, and in less than one hundred years it too had to be replaced, this time with more durable stone from Derbyshire. This third façade, however, is a perfect copy of the original front.

The chantry was occupied in medieval times by a chaplain who received alms from wayfarers and who in return prayed for a safe continuation of their journey. After the building became disused in the seventeenth century it served successively as a corn store office, an old clothes shop, a library, a newsroom, and cheese cake shop. Its ecclesiastical use was then restored and a service is held within its sacred walls on Sunday afternoons.

CHAPTER II

Airedale—Goole to Malham

No English river presents greater contrasts than the Aire. The headwaters around Malham are enclosed by impressive scenery which has inspired novelists and poets, including John Ruskin and Charles Kingsley. Part of *The Water Babies* was written by Kingsley while he was a guest of the millionaire Walter Morrison at Malham Tarn House. Another illustrious visitor to that remote residence was Charles Darwin, who found the lonely setting conducive to his studies.

Kingsley was so enchanted by the fishing potential of the Tarn (the source of the Aire) that he declared it 'the best fishing on the earth'—clearly an exaggeration, but a statement cherished by all who know the upper reaches of Airedale.

This happy picture continues downstream as far as Skipton before a more sombre one starts to build up. The change is more evident at Keighley, where effluents pollute the stream. Thenceforward the deterioration increases as the Aire winds through the industrial region of the West Riding.

Bingley, Shipley, Esholt, Leeds and Castleford, each has a part in this unwelcome change, which only finishes when the Aire reaches its outfall into the Ouse near Goole. These places contribute to the condition in which few freshwater creatures can survive.

The situation is not regarded as irreversible, and improvements which can only be described as startling are promised for the next decade. The Aire is one of the rivers chosen to be restored under the National River Survey, the aim being to bring it back to a standard that will enable its water to be used for general industrial purposes.

Already there have been experiments in re-using some of the effluent from Pudsey in textile processes, and re-cycling in that way is said to be promising. A further step will be to make fishing and boating possible where they cannot be carried out at present. Leeds

Mastiles Lane, linking Malham and Kilnsey.

has put forward plans for a boating venue and marina near the centre of the city.

Goole, where the Aire and Ouse merge, has become an important port only during the last one hundred years, but there is nearby a cutting known as the Dutch River in honour of Sir Cornelius Vermuyden, the genius from Holland who was engaged by Charles I to drain the submerged land hereabouts and make it habitable and fertile. As recompense for this stupendous feat Vermuyden was to receive one-third of the reclaimed area, another third was to be public property, and the king was to receive the remainder.

The task was carried out successfully, but not without opposition. The local populace complained, perhaps justifiably, that the scheme caused the flooding of land which they had already drained and cultivated. Several Dutchmen were killed in riots, but the project was finished in 1635. During the Civil War the local inhabitants sided with the Roundheads, and when Royalists massed to take over the area the natives resisted vigorously. They seized the part owned by Vermuyden and fell upon the colonists he had introduced from the Netherlands. Their crops were destroyed by driving cattle across the fields, sluices were opened to inundate the district, and embankments were torn down.

Rawcliffe, a village gathered round a tree-shaded green on the Aire four miles from Goole, was the home of one of Yorkshire's eccentrics a century after Civil War days. Jimmy (or Jemmy) Hurst was born at this place in 1738, and one of his oddities in early manhood was to ride to market on a bull which he called Jupiter. He also trained the animal to hunt with the hounds.

His clothing was no less extraordinary. He sported a red jacket with blue sleeves, blue breeches, a waistcoat made of drakes' necks with the feathers outside, crimson stockings, yellow shoes with big silver buckles, and a lambskin hat 9 feet around the brim. Thus dressed, Jimmy rode around a wide area in a carriage which resembled a Chinese hat on wheels. The vehicle was drawn by Jupiter and became a familiar sight not only around Rawcliffe but much farther afield as well.

Aristocrats went miles out of their way to visit his home, and they carried his fame to London. When George III heard about this singular Yorkshireman, Jimmy was summoned to the royal court. He drove south in his curious carriage, attracting crowds of sightseers on the way. Court procedure meant little to him, and instead of kissing the monarch's hand on bowed knee, he stood up and gave him a hearty handshake, also expressing surprise on finding the king 'such a plain, homely old gentleman' whom he would like to entertain at Rawcliffe.

There is little doubt that, had the streets of London really been made of gold slabs, Jimmy Hurst would have profited from them. Despite his eccentricities he was an astute businessman. When he inherited £1,000 from his father he soon turned it into £6,000 by speculating in corn, potatoes, and flax.

The cottage which he occupied was burnt after his death in 1829. Another house was built on the site, however, and for many years the villagers of Rawcliffe attracted tourists by wrongly pointing out this later dwelling as Jimmy's home.

Leeds may have derived its name from a Flanders township called Leedes, known to the Saxons who came to England some fifteen hundred years ago. Strangely enough, a village near the continental Leedes is called Holbeck, and the Yorkshire city of Leeds has a district bearing that title.

Some historians, however, suggest that the city takes its name from 'Caer Loidis Coit', a town in a wood. A third theory is that the first Saxon to be overlord of the site was Loidi, and that Leeds perpetuates his personal name. The Romans knew this locality too, many relics of their occupation having been unearthed thereabouts. It is thought that one of their connecting roads followed the line of the Leeds thoroughfare called Briggate.

Whatever the truth on those matters, the city did not receive its first charter of incorporation until 1626, and not until 1832 did Leeds become entitled to have its own M.P.

During the Civil War the populace supported the Parliamentarians, but Royalist forces overcame them and remained until Roundhead troops ousted them in January 1643.

Charles I was lodged in Leeds as a captive on his way to London, and an engaging account says that a Leeds maidservant volunteered to show him a way of escape. Though he refused to thwart his jailers he gave the maid a token, telling her that if she showed it to him later, or to his son, she would receive a good reward. And so she did, Charles II honouring the pact and promoting her husband from under-bailiff in Leeds to the post of chief bailiff for all Yorkshire.

Leeds is not particularly well endowed with historic treasures, but it has strong links with Mary Queen of Scots, her husband Lord Darnley having been born at Temple Newsham House, the splendid brick-built mansion which became Leeds citizens' property in 1922 as a result of great generosity by Lord Halifax.

Nor does the city today forget its famous sons. Statues of some of them look across City Square. Represented there are James Watt, Joseph Priestley, who discovered oxygen, and Dean Hook, another distinguished cleric.

Matthew Murray stands with them as a leading designer of steam locomotives. His figure is especially apt, for Leeds also cherishes the oldest working railway in the world. It was established in 1758 for colliery use, and is now preserved and operated by the Middleton Railway Trust.

Another famous name connected with Leeds is that of Captain Oates, companion of Captain Scott the South Pole explorer. Oates was a resident of Meanwood, a Leeds suburb, and a plaque recording his heroism has been placed on the gateway of the parish church there.

And where else in the realm, except at a spot near the River Aire outside Leeds, can you see an industry which has functioned continuously and on the same site since it was founded by Cistercian monks eight hundred years or so ago? The honour goes to the engineering works known as Kirkstall Forge.

Kirkstall Abbey, still impressive in its ruined state, rivalled Fountains Abbey in its heyday as a Cistercian retreat. Its founders came from Barnoldswick to escape harassment, and were befriended by Henry de Lacy, a Norman baron suffering from a distressing illness. He vowed that if he recovered he would enable the monks from the Lancashire-Yorkshire border area to erect a monastery beside the River Aire at Kirkstall.

That was in the year 1147, and during successive decades their church was extended, making it complete in about thirty years. A point worth noting is that throughout the period the Kirkstall monks were often in financial straits, and were unable to decorate the architecture to the extent carried out in other Cistercian abbeys.

Consequently Kirkstall retained its main features unaltered, and with minor exceptions the structure we visit today is the work of one period. The entire buildings are clearly of the same uniform type.

One exception is the tower, originally a squat feature only a little higher than the main roof. It conformed with the early Cistercian dictum that towers were a symbol of pride and vanity, and should not be really lofty. But this rule was eventually relaxed, and in the fifteenth century the Kirkstall tower was raised to its present height.

In four hundred years the monks of Kirkstall became a rich community, owning agricultural land and grazing areas far away. When Henry VIII confiscated the monasteries, this one in Airedale had annual revenues equal to £50,000 in present-day money.

Archbishop Cranmer was granted the estate, and after a number of other transactions it was acquired by the Earl of Cardigan. In 1889 the property was bought by a Leeds native, Colonel North, then living in Kent. He gave the Abbey to the Corporation of Leeds, who have since undertaken its preservation. Excavations have also been carried out to reveal the outlines of the various sections, and the grounds as well as the buildings have become a public haven.

The Aire skirts Bradford, favouring a route nearer Shipley and Saltaire, and the city has recently lost many of its highly presentable Victorian buildings at the behest of 'progress'. Its tall roofed market hall has had to accept defeat by planners who have opted for a replacement in the modern box-style architecture. The ornate Swan Arcade, comprised of many small offices where textile dealers followed their trade, has also been demolished.

The Wool Exchange, long a monopoly as a meeting-place for wool merchants, is no longer regarded as sacrosanct against other kinds of business. How some of the departed would squirm if they were to know that parts of the building have been converted into shops.

Saltaire and its history have an outstanding place in the development of the textile industry. Here was carried out the first project to provide homes as well as employment for factory workers. In short, this spot was the first site in the country to have a 'model' township.

Its founder, Sir Titus Salt, built it on about twenty-six acres and erected some three hundred dwellings, mostly in a uniform style, and various other buildings. But he stipulated that no public houses were to be included, for he was a strict teetotaller. Some odd rules were imposed on domestic activities, too. Thus there were restrictions on the use of washing lines, the indiscriminate hanging of laundry out of doors being considered detrimental to the appearance of the estate.

In Victoria Road, the main route to Saltaire Mills, is evidence of another of Sir Titus's whims. On a business visit to London he heard that four carved stone lions originally intended for Trafalgar Square had been rejected because they were regarded as too small for that site.

The business magnate from Airedale, however, considered that they were eminently suitable for Saltaire. He bought them and had them set up in Victoria Road. There they stand today, mute creatures which failed to measure up to their intended role at the base of Nelson's Column.

The animal statues are said to have been modelled after real lions in the Regents Park Zoo by Thomas Milnes, but when his work was examined by the committee concerned, they contracted Sir Edwin Landseer to provide bigger leonine figures.

Those at Saltaire weigh nearly three tons each, and are named respectively Vigilance, Determination, Peace, and War. The transfer of the contract to Landseer was not completely successful. He failed to deliver the lions promptly, despite pressure, and they were not ready for unveiling until 1868, more than a quarter of a century after the transformation of the rest of Trafalgar Square.

At Baildon, which dominates the landscape between Shipley and the fringe of Ilkley, is a churchyard epitaph to a reformer described as having been directly responsible for the introduction of the parcels post service. His tombstone also refers to him as the pioneer of the Old Age Pensions scheme.

It was Alexander Atkinson's agitation for the latter which earned him the nickname 'Pensions Atkinson' and prompted him to tour business offices, public houses, and other premises, expounding his ideas to anyone who would listen.

An unusual figure in top hat and morning suit, he carried a half-rolled umbrella, and was a familiar character in the Bradford area. During the first few years of the present century he was always ready to produce from his black bag a wealth of documents to support whatever cause he was publicising at the moment.

He put forward figures and facts which, he claimed, would make a parcel post service as helpful and popular as the cheap letter post already was. He is reputed to have persuaded the Postmaster General to adopt the idea.

His Old Age Pension scheme was based on a plan for a central fund of £1 million, half obtained by a weekly levy of one penny on rents and the balance provided by the Exchequer. This money, Alexander Atkinson calculated, would enable everybody over sixty to receive eight shillings a week from the State.

During his career as a political reformer this Baildonian himself lived on next to nothing, being supported by his family and gratuities. Although his activities brought him notoriety rather than fame when he was alive, he was esteemed enough to have his work for his fellow men commemorated by the gravestone inscription in the parish churchyard at Baildon, where he was buried in December 1907, at the age of sixty-seven.

Bingley, six miles from Bradford, has been called 'The Throstle Nest of Old England' and it has striven to retain that status despite the growth of industry and the heavy weight of road traffic passing along the main street.

Adjoining the Bingley–Harden road are sylvan scenes comparable with some of the most admired beauty spots in Britain. The lovely St. Ives estate was chosen for the setting for scientific work by the Sports Turf Research Institute, where problems of turf management are investigated. Various types of grass are grown in small plots near the mansion on the estate, and samples of turf, pests, and other sportsground features are sent there from all over the world. Experts from this centre also make personal visits, taking first hand help to sports clubs needing advice about their grounds.

The mansion now serving as the focal point of the research was long owned and occupied by the Ferrands, one of the leading families in the Bingley district. An inscription on a stone incorporated in the oldest part of the building reads:

> If thou a house shalt finde
> built to thy minde,
> And that without thy cost,
> Serve thou the more,
> God and the poore,
> And then thy labour is not lost.

There is some uncertainty about the origin of these lines but they are commonly believed to have been placed on the house at the instigation of Lady Anne Clifford, the Skipton benefactress. She was a patron for the erection of the old St. Ives house.

Two other inscribed references to the Ferrands survive, both of them near the adjoining moor. One is an obelisk 'affectionately dedicated' to William Ferrand, Knaresborough M.P. for fifteen years. He was an active supporter of the Ten Hours' Factory Bill, as well as a ceaseless agitator for the abolition of the Truck System. He was largely instrumental for the introduction of legislation compelling employers to pay wages in cash and not in goods.

Near Stockbridge, on the outskirts of Keighley, the Aire makes a wide loop, and tradition says that it originally flowed nearer East Riddlesden Hall, but it made a detour to get as far away as possible from the Hall when the Murgatroyds and Rishworths lived there and led dissolute lives.

Today this seventeenth century manor house is National Trust property, having been given to that body by two Keighley philanthropists in 1934. The acquisition included a fishpond and two old barns. The huge barn overlooking the pond is one of the finest medieval farm buildings in the country. Its interior resembles the inside of a church, with aisles, and the door is studded.

On the East Riddlesden estate was bred the celebrated Airedale Heifer. She measured 11 feet 10 inches in length and weighed $41\frac{3}{4}$ stones per quarter. Plans were made to exhibit the animal, but she

Haworth Parsonage, home of the Brontës.

suffered an accident and had to be destroyed before the tour could
be started.

Keighley has not much of historic importance for visitors. It is,
however, a gateway to Haworth and the Brontë country, and in
recent years it has added a new attraction, the re-born Worth
Valley Railway.

There is no more enjoyable way of approaching Haworth than by
boarding one of the restored passenger coaches at Keighley Station
and being drawn to the capital of Brontëland by a steam locomotive.

Haworth has things to show which are unconnected with the
Brontes or only slightly so. One such object is an old font on a
pedestal in the parish churchyard. It bears the inscription WM.
GRIMSHAW—A. B. MINISTER—AD 1742.

The relic is a reminder that before the Brontes arrived at
Haworth the spiritual wellbeing of the inhabitants was looked after
by a cleric of widespread renown. In earlier benefices Grimshaw
gained a reputation for gay living, but religious experiences during
his early days in this Worth Valley parish caused him to repent
and become a most earnest disciple and a powerful preacher.

His commanding figure was respected by the law-abiding and feared by the law-breakers. On Sunday mornings he toured the local inns and used a whip to drive out any parishioners he found there, herding them to church.

He may be regarded as a pioneer of Church Unity, giving his support to other denominations than the Church of England. Haworth's first Methodist chapel was founded during his ministry in the village, and he gave the sponsors his blessing. Haworth's earliest Baptist community was begun by one of Grimshaw's own lay preachers, and Grimshaw expressly provided for his own funeral sermon to be given by a Methodist Minister.

The parish church itself has an oddity in its tower, though few visitors observe that one of the four clock dials differs from the others.

This singularity arises because in 1934 a severe gale dislodged the dial on the west side and sent it crashing down on to the pavement below, smashing it beyond repair. The existing clock face on that side is a replacement fitted six months later. Unlike the old dial, which was made of cast iron and weighed fifteen hundredweights, the new one is copper plate. Although it is about the same size (8 feet 4 inches across), it is much lighter in weight.

CHAPTER III

Keighley to Malham

North-westwards from Keighley, Airedale begins to adopt the characteristic drystone walls of the Pennines. The limestone of the region lends itself admirably to the building of walls without mortar, and such walls form a complicated pattern across the higher reaches of the Dale.

It is durable enough to withstand the vagaries of the weather for decades, yet it can be more easily chipped to shape than many other kinds of stone. In fact the expert drywaller often uses no tool other than a hammer to shape the stones, chipping off only small pieces and making a good job largely by exercising a keen eye for selecting his material, thereby minimising the need for tooling.

Another secret of the craft is to use 'throughs'—big, carefully picked stones which will go right through the wall to form a secure base for the smaller stones. The hallmark of a good mortarless wall is the number of 'throughs' it contains and the positions they occupy.

A practised workman can build in a day 20 to 30 feet of dry stone walling 1 foot 6 inches wide and 4 feet 6 inches high. These measurements, however, are not the maximum dimensions of such walls. Some rise to 6 feet and are nearly 3 feet wide.

Some of the examples existing today may well have been built originally by laymen employed by the monasteries. The monks and canons of such retreats as Fountains Abbey, Bolton Priory, and other monastic places grazed big flocks of sheep on the Yorkshire fells. Some of the routes along which the flocks were driven remain today as green roads flanked by drystone walls.

Fears that the craft of building this style of boundary walling was dying out completely have been allayed in recent years. Contests to continue interest in the work have been included in some of the annual agricultural and livestock shows held in the dales, notably at Kilnsey, Wharfedale.

Again, road development schemes have necessitated setting back the border walls, and in appropriate instances they have been rebuilt in the old-fashioned way, thus not only helping to preserve the medieval craft but retaining the old appearance of the landscape.

One curious custom associated with drywalling today, however, has lapsed. The workmen in bygone days used to throw their hammer before starting each stint. Where the hammer landed was accepted as showing the length of wall they were to build before nightfall.

The present-day drywaller works to more definite standards, and is usually paid according to the time he takes, rather than in relation to the length of wall he constructs.

In addition to grazing sheep on the Yorkshire fells, the monks provided bridges for the shepherds and cattle drovers, where they needed to cross rivers. One such point was at Kildwick, five miles from Keighley, and an astonishing survival from those times is the bridge spanning the Aire near the village. It is astonishing because no drastic alterations have been made to the structure, though it carries an ever-increasing amount of road traffic. Nor has it failed to withstand the battering it receives from today's heavy vehicles, a

Kildwick Bridge, between Skipton and Keighley.

usage certainly never envisaged by its founders, the canons of Bolton Priory.

The bridge is probably the one mentioned in the Priory accounts for the years 1305 and 1306, when £21 12s. 9d. was recorded as having been spent on the construction of Kildwick Bridge. It was narrower than the present width, but the original piers can be seen beneath it. Widening took place in 1780, when the four eastern arches were rounded instead of being arched. Two of the arches on the western side are still in the original arched form. But the river no longer flows under them; they have been retained to obviate the steep gradient which would otherwise have been needed. The width between the parapets is still only 23 feet, and this bridge must rank as one of the most interesting in Yorkshire, if not the finest.

Kildwick Church, on the northern bank of the river, has other links with Bolton Priory. Until 1825 the church contained a splendid oak canopy to cover the font, this canopy being given by the canons of Bolton. In the year mentioned, the erection of a west gallery necessitated the removal of the canopy. It was subsequently cut up and a cabinetmaker used the wood for chairs!

A souvenir from the heydays of Bolton Priory nevertheless survives in the form of a modern tomb bearing the magnificent recumbent figure of Sir Robert de Stiveton, a member of a highly esteemed Steeton family. He died in 1307, and the canons of Bolton admired him to such a degree that they had this effigy of him placed in Kildwick Church.

It represents Sir Robert in the garb of a Knight Templar, and it is especially important as an historic memorial because it must have been one of the last funeral figures so attired, the military religious Order having been suppressed soon afterwards.

Nearer our own time is a framed letter written by Florence Nightingale at Scutari in Asia Minor, thanking the inhabitants of Kildwick for supporting her work in the Crimea.

This Airedale church has a further claim to distinction. It has a length of 176 feet and is $48\frac{1}{2}$ feet wide, making it the longest village church in the county, exceeding by 4 feet the length of a rival, Snaith church near Selby. The parish registers at Kildwick are exceptional for the hundreds of entries recording payments for the destruction of foxes, hedgehogs, kites, hawks, otters and other creatures classed as vermin. The entries were begun in 1669 and also include 1s. 6d. paid to the bellringers in November 1746 for pealing the end of the 1745 Rebellion.

Alongside the road between Kildwick and Skipton is a stretch of the Leeds and Liverpool Canal, a project officially begun in 1766 with the support of the famous civil engineer James Brindley. The Bingley–Skipton section was opened seven years later, becoming part of a grandiose scheme to thrust a canal across the Pennines.

Skipton High Street is dominated by a castle which, contrary to many of our ancient fortresses, is not ruinous but still includes occupied apartments. A home of the baronial Cliffords, its preservation would have delighted Anne Clifford, the eccentric benefactress who lived here and had the castle restored after it was damaged in the Civil War. Characteristically she gave priority to the repair of the adjoining parish church, which contains important emblazoned monuments to earlier Cliffords.

There are memories of another member of the family in the imposing gatehouse. Here is a chamber decorated with countless sea shells brought to this part of Yorkshire by the buccaneering

Skipton Castle.

Earl of Cumberland from distant parts of the world. The parapet of the archway bears the family motto, 'Desormais' (Hereafter) made up of carved stone letters.

It was through this portal that in December 1645 marched Royalists, surrendering to Parliamentarian troops. Although the castle had just undergone a three years' siege, its defenders did not emerge abjectly, but in an orderly fashion with colours flying, trumpets sounding, and drums beating. They were also allowed to carry their weapons, with powder and bullets, though it was stipulated that no foot soldier should march away with any baggage.

The parish church, beautifully restored by the Countess of Cumberland, and bearing her initials on various features, contains the huge tomb of the Sailor Earl. It is one of the most surprising treasures in the country, being decorated with coloured heraldry showing the Clifford line of descent and the connections of the family with other illustrious ones.

Christ Church, beside the road from Kildwick and Keighley, gives the visitor to Skipton something else to see. An upright grave-stone in the churchyard is inscribed with a reference to 'General Tom Thumb'. The Skipton bearer of that name, however, was not the celebrated Charles Stratton who was exhibited in London more than a century ago and received that military title unofficially. The Skipton midget was a local dwarf named after the much better-known dwarf as a courtesy. When other vertical tombstones were uprooted and placed elsewhere to improve the appearance of the churchyard, a few years ago, this intriguing slab was allowed to stay upright on its original site.

Skipton is known as the Gateway to the Craven Country, the Craeg Van or land of crags as it was called in Saxon times. The region, stretching to Malham and beyond, is still an unspoiled area in that category, having such spectacular limestone features as Malham Cove and Gordale Scar.

The Scar, one of the most awe-inspiring wonders in the country, is about one mile east of Malham village. It is in fact a great cavern which has lost its roof, and is made all the more startling to visitors because it is burst upon suddenly on rounding a bend in the valley. On the left are overhanging cliffs towering to 300 feet, and into the abyss plunges Gordale Beck, a particularly impressive sight after a period of heavy rain.

At such times the falling water creates a thunderous roar which is increased by echoing and re-echoing from the cliffs. On these occasions the scene and sounds are considered to exceed in grandeur the famous cataract of Lodore in Cumberland.

In point of fact this Gordale spectacle is not the one which thrilled sightseers before the year 1730. A terrific thunderstorm in that year diverted the stream from its original route near the centre of the pass and caused it to burst the rocky barrier through which it emerges today.

Malham Cove lacks the chilling atmosphere of Gordale Scar, although it is of similar height and was created in the same way by an immense convulsion when Airedale was being formed. The Cove, a giant amphitheatre, is nonetheless of intense interest for it contains a mystery.

On the plateau above this geological marvel is Malham Tarn, 1,250 feet above sea level and covering 160 acres. Some three miles north of the village, this stretch of water is regarded as the source of the Aire.

But the stream issuing from the tarn vanishes into 'swallow holes' before reaching the brink of the Cove, and reappears at the foot of the amphitheatre. An unanswered question is how it comes about that two springs half a mile below Malham village receive water from the tarn more quickly than the stream emerging from the base of the Cove, whenever a flood occurs.

The strange circumstance gives rise to a belief that some big natural syphoning system operates within the Cove, or that the passage to the springs is comparatively straight, whereas the route from the tarn to the foot of the Cove includes a series of high waterfalls behind the limestone face, these cascades dropping into deep or extensive pools hidden from view.

The Craven area is also the domain of cave explorers, or pot-holers, whose pursuit is nowadays widely popular. Numerous subterranean passages in the region challenge speliologists to make carefully planned descents into underground Yorkshire. Some of the most accessible caves have been entered by ordinary sightseers, although the real netherworld presents many hazards and is the true realm of expert explorers.

The practice of penetrating deep into underground Yorkshire may be said to have originated in the 1840s, when an intrepid team of ten persons ventured into Alum Pot, near Horton-in-Ribblesdale. Caving was also promoted when a Frenchman, M. Martel, succeeded in fathoming Gaping Ghyll Hole, and got to the floor of this immense chamber inside the east flank of Ingleborough.

That was in 1895, and this cave has since become something of a showplace. From time to time members of the ordinary public are enabled to go down the shaft in a bosun's chair lowered and raised by a windlass, after the stream which normally plunges down the pothole has been diverted.

They reach a vast subterranean hall which could contain London's Albert Hall. The stream, before its course is altered to eject it into another pothole nearby, hurtles over the brink of Gaping Ghyll Hole to become the highest waterfall known to exist anywhere in Britain.

Other cave systems inside the Pennines have been turned into everyday tourist attractions. In this category are Ingleborough Cave near Clapham, and White Scar Caverns near Pateley Bridge, Nidderdale.

But exploring more difficult passages and caves in north-west Yorkshire is more than just a means of experiencing new thrills. It is adding to our knowledge of life in this county before the beginnings of recorded history. Objects found by cavers have included the bones of grizzly bears, bison, reindeer, hyenas, hippopotami, elephants, and mammoths—all creatures long extinct in Britain but which obviously once lived here.

Remains of this sort, together with pottery, Roman-Celtic coins, amber and glass beads, silver and gold-plated bronze brooches, finger rings and other ornaments of great beauty have come to light in Victoria Cave, Settle. Their discovery has revealed that a race inhabited this cave in far distant times, and that these people were by no means primitive.

Settle, the nearest market centre to this cavern, is on the Ribble, which later flows through Lancashire. A monster backcloth to the town is the massive bulk of Castleberg, a lofty limestone scar forming a bastion on the northern side. Only the top of the old market cross has survived (it now terminates the column over the drinking fountain in the market square) but some engaging architecture is to be seen around the town.

The Shambles behind the market cross consist of a series of arches occupied by shops and bearing two-storeyed properties overlooked by Castleberg.

Foreign to the Dales, too, is the extensive Tanner House, more

Settle—market place, with the Shambles.

often called The Folly, off the market place. Its originator was Sir Thomas Preston, and its bizarre appearance justifies its colloquial name given to it soon after it was built in 1675.

On the southern side of the market place, on premises which were once an inn, is to be seen the Naked Man sign of that port of call. Just how it came to have so singular a name is uncertain, but disinterest in current modes of dress indeed was encouraged hereabouts by local regulations, one exacting a toll for each new hat worn on market days. A further factor, the legal requirement to pay a fine if a cap of English-knit wool was not worn on Sundays and Holy Days, may have had a bearing on Settle folks' reputation for dowdiness. In these circumstances it would have been considered improvident to pay much attention to fashionable attire.

Nor were other ways of making the inhabitants presentable to visitors given endorsement by the religious authorities in Settle. As recently as the late nineteenth century, it was considered sinful there to use pomade, and sermons denouncing the practice as evil were preached in local chapels.

Settle parish church became a centenarian in 1938, and thus has little of historical interest, but it was built just in time to serve as a memorial church for navvies killed during the construction of the nearby Settle–Carlisle railway.

Ecclesiastically the town has long been attached to the much older church at Giggleswick on the other bank of the Ribble. This edifice has much more to entice the tourists, having been erected in the reign of Henry VII, a great church building era.

An outstanding possession is a great reading desk carved with the names and symbols of the tribes of Israel. The front of the desk carries the carved message 'Hear is the standards of the Israelites when they to Canan cam agenst the Cananites'. This splendid piece of furniture was made in 1680 and bears the initials of the church-wardens of that time and a carved representation of three collecting boxes.

A most remarkable discovery was made during restoration of this church towards the close of the last century. A statue of a fifteenth century knight, Sir Richard Tempest, was unearthed, but a more astonishing revelation was that his warhorse was buried with him, an unusual gesture showing the affection between a soldier and his mount.

The village cross, just outside the churchyard, is thought by some historians to incorporate the main part of the old one at Settle, which dated from the reign of Henry III. The Settle pillar is believed to have been removed surreptitiously to Giggleswick when the inhabitants of the village wanted to substantiate a claim concerning the antiquity of their own market.

The domed building visible from the village is part of the famous Giggleswick grammar school, one of the oldest and most opulent institutions of its kind in the country. Founded in 1507 by James Carr, whose family were connected with Furness Abbey, Lancashire, in 1552 the school was more richly endowed by John Nowell, vicar of Giggleswick. At that time he was chaplain to the young King Edward VI.

Down the years this Dales institution has had many names of distinction on its registers, including the eminent Very Rev. John S. Howson, nineteenth century Dean of Chester, Dr. George Birkbeck, founder of Mechanics' Institutes, and Dr. Abraham Sutcliffe, founder of the Medical Society of London, who is also credited with having introduced that widely useful root, the mangel-wurzel, into Britain to the great benefit of farmers needing food for cattle.

Did these celebrated scholars participate in an old schoolboy custom observed at Gigglewick, paying visits to the ebbing well at the foot of Buckhaw Brow to obtain water for liquorice drinks? The well-water was considered to be the best for dissolving the plant root.

The chief phenomenon of this spring, however, is the manner in which it gradually fills and then suddenly depletes the contents of the stone basin, a peculiar action which has been noted for generations. The flowing and ebbing ordinarily occurs each seven or eight minutes, but it does not take place at times of flood or drought.

Various explanations have been put forward to account for this strange movement, including the patently absurd idea that tidal movements on the North Lancashire coast were transmitted to the basin along some underground channels. More tenable is the suggestion that some syphoning operation is performed between two cavities behind the well.

It is hard to realise that the Pennines around Ingleton were thickly forested until the time of the Roman occupation, with only the barren summits of the mountains peeping through the trees. The ancient Britons dwelt only on the top of these heights, where

Ingleborough, West Riding

traces of their horse-shoe shaped habitations have been found.

On the bleak summit of Ingleborough they lit fires to worship their gods and keep at bay the wild creatures which infested the forests below. The trees were not cleared until the legions from Rome invaded the Craven area in the first century AD and cut down the forests in order to control the resident tribes.

The present church at Ingleton is historically unremarkable, the fabric being less than one hundred years old, excepting the fifteenth century tower. The most prized possession is the Norman font, circular in shape and elaborately carved with illustrations from the life of Christ.

It is a miracle that this treasured relic has survived at all, for in Commonwealth days it was considered idolatrous and was thrown into the nearby River Greta. On another occasion it was used as a mixing trough for mortar, and became thickly encrusted with lime. It was also made to serve as a whitewash bowl when the interior of the church was being treated.

CHAPTER IV

Along and Around the Don

In this chapter we follow the course of the Don for seventy miles through the West Riding from the point a few miles south of Holmfirth where it rises, near the borders of Cheshire and Derbyshire, until it flows into the Dutch Canal on the way to Goole.

Soon after its birth the stream is joined by the so-called Little Don at Deepcar and thereafter accompanies the main Huddersfield–Sheffield road through Wharncliffe Chase, an area of superb beauty and enchanting woodland walks.

Our armchair journey will touch Sheffield, Rotherham, and Doncaster, and will make at least a nodding acquaintance with various smaller places meriting attention—Thorne, Fishlake, Hatfield, Arksey, Sprotbrough, Warmsworth, Conisborough, Hooton Pagnell, Hooton Roberts, Midhopestones, and Langsett.

Marsden, six miles from Holmfirth, does not forget that one of its sons gained fame as a Lancashire poet, and was widely called the 'Lancashire Rhymer', despite his Yorkshire birth and early upbringing. Samuel Laycock was born in Marsden in 1826, and before moving to Lancashire worked in a textile factory on the Yorkshire side of the Pennines.

Later he wrote verses which reflected the conditions prevailing in Yorkshire factories a century ago. His mill experience inspired poems with a homely appeal, epitomising the lives led by workers during the Industrial Revolution.

Laycock is said to have been encouraged by Edwin Waugh, the 'Lancashire Burns', who was his contemporary. In those days it was customary for poets to have their verses printed in sheet form, the copies then being peddled by the poets personally in market places and from door to door.

Laycock hired a stall in Oldham market as a sales centre, selling his lyrics at one penny a sheet. In this way he sold forty thousand sheets before they were collected and published in book form. His best known poem is the one ending with the line 'It's cappin' sometimes what a 'awpny will do'. His 'Bonny Brid' is still a favourite for recitations by the older generation.

'Learn or leave' was the motto of a grammar school which functioned at Penistone for six hundred years. The curriculum at one period included instruction in hunting deer, and the scholars once had the regular job of policing the district against 'nightly perils'.

Among the pupils was the blind Nicholas Saunderson, later Professor of Mathematics at Cambridge, a close friend of Sir Isaac Newton. The sightless Penistone scholar is said to have taught himself to identify and learn the letters of the alphabet by running his fingers over inscriptions on the tombstones in the churchyard.

The tower of Penistone Church has a double at Silkstone in the same neighbourhood, both towers having been designed by the same architect. He used the same plans for both and the structures are identical except in minor details.

Sheffield inhabitants know Wharncliffe Crags and Woods as a delightful retreat within easy reach of the city. The crags form natural terraces and viewpoints for surveying the area, and through this tree-girt valley the Don flows on its way to the centre of steel-making.

The great chase of Wharncliffe was considered to be the finest area in the county for deer hunting before collieries and ironstone mines defiled the vicinity.

An unwelcome denizen of the rocks below the terraces was the Dragon of Wantley, a fearsome legendary creature which devoured all the trees surrounding its lair, sparing the rocks only because they were too hard for him to crack.

This monster was eventually slain by a man wearing a spiked suit of armour specially made at Sheffield. Tradition continues that the making of this special suit of metal was the origin of Sheffield's industry. Wharncliffe has some literary distinction too, being referred to in *Ivanhoe*. Sir Walter Scott describes the locality as 'That pleasant district of Merry England watered by the river Don'.

Visitors will find the towering Table Rock an enticement today, for it is claimed that on a clear day the towers of York Minster and Lincoln Cathedral are visible from its summit.

A grim souvenir adjoins the churchyard at Bradfield, an otherwise pleasant village west of the Don near Oughtibridge. Here is a watch-house where a vigil was kept after burials to thwart the bodysnatchers who dug up recently buried corpses and sold them to medical schools for dissection.

Lake-like reservoirs close at hand are now an attractive feature of the landscape, constructed for the more practical purpose of meeting Sheffield's thirst for water. In 1864, however, they brought tragedy to Low Bradfield and a number of other places on the way to that city, one of the man-made lakes bursting its banks and sending millions of gallons of water surging down the dale.

The torrent swept houses aside, demolished mills, breached bridges and drowned over two hundred people. It was a repetition of the great flood which had struck Holmfirth eighteen years earlier, when a reservoir in that area broke its banks and released a torrent which drowned the town while its inhabitants slept.

Modern Sheffield is the largest city in Yorkshire, and the fifth largest in England. It has been transformed since the end of the Second World War. Far from being the grimy, blackened and smoky place of pre-war days, it now presents itself as the cleanest industrial city in Britain—and, say some people, in all Europe— thanks to smoke control measures and their strict application.

On the other hand the city and its environs are by no means devoid of historic treasures, and mementoes of the men who made it famous. In Sheffield Cathedral a picture in stained glass portrays the clockmaker of German parentage whose foresight made him the pioneer of the city's steelworks. He was Benjamin Huntsman, a Quaker who needed steel for his timepieces. He exercised his genius by experimenting with various processes until he finally found one which met his meticulous requirements.

The steel he produced was better than the products marketed by the Sheffield metallurgists of his day, but the cutlers to whom he offered it refused to buy from him, and he had to export his metal. Foreign competition later forced the cutlers to reconsider their attitude, but instead of turning to Benjamin Huntsman for their supplies they spied on his workmen in an effort to discover what made his steel so superior.

Many tricks were tried to obtain this secret, but Huntsman was alert and no stranger was ever allowed in the works. His precautions were finally thwarted by a bogus tramp named Walker, who turned up at the gate shivering with cold and pleading to sleep beside a fire which heated one of the crucibles.

Sheffield—Fargate Shopping Precinct.

The tramp watched Huntsman's workmen and followed their process through half-closed eyes.

Huntsman's foundry still survives on the Bakewell Road as an industrial museum. Here can be seen one of the furnaces he developed in 1742 for steel which was beaten into scythes by tilt hammers worked by water power.

Further back in history, Mary Queen of Scots was held as a prisoner at Sheffield for fourteen years. Her jail was the castle of the Earls of Shrewsbury. George Talbot, the sixth in that line was given the responsibility of keeping her in custody. The fortress has disappeared, but a building known as the Turret House still stands. It provided the queen with a more pleasant outlook than the castle itself, and one of her 'treats' was to climb the winding stairway to admire the landscape which surrounded Sheffield in Tudor times.

A priceless possession of the city is an early autograph album made up of 187 leaves of vellum. It contains exquisite miniatures in gold, blue, crimson, and green, but its most precious feature is an entry signed 'Mary Queen of France and Scots'.

There are a number of monuments in Sheffield Cathedral, a cruciform building partly rebuilt after bomb damage in the Second World War, so great and varied that only brief details can be given here. But most of these memorials, and the lives of the individuals they represent, merit diligent study.

The composer, Sir William Sterndale Bennett, a Sheffield man by birth, has a monument to him with two bars of his musical setting for 'God is a spirit'. He knew the cathedral in his boyhood, before it was elevated to its present ecclesiastical status in 1913.

In Saxon times Earl Waltheof, Lord of Hallamshire (an area comprising the parishes of Sheffield and Ecclesfield) resisted the Norman invasion of 1066 but married a niece of the Conqueror when the Saxons were defeated. The earl thus saved his own life, but only temporarily. Accused of treachery by the Conqueror he was executed at Winchester in 1075.

His name was revered by the Saxons, however, especially after they learned that information about his deceit had been passed by his estranged wife to the Norman sovereign. Nor does Sheffield forget him. The Cathedral shows his likeness in stained glass.

Pictures in glass also draw attention to Cardinal Wolsey, who was held at Sheffield after his arrest at Cawood near Selby.

Other reminders of men who made Sheffield the important city it is today, by introducing trade or promoting the steel industry by developing new processes, exist in and around the late nineteenth century Town Hall and the Cutlers Hall. James Watt, Stephenson, Davy, Faraday, Wheatstone and Swan are commemorated by having their names on a scroll of fame held by figures symbolising Steam and Electricity on the front of the former building.

The Cutlers Hall, an impressive building opened in 1832, serves as the headquarters of the seventeenth century Company of Cutlers, a guild founded to protect the interests of cutlers in this part of Yorkshire and North Derbyshire. The Company still makes use of the right to register trade marks, a privilege granted by Act of Parliament in 1624.

The present Hall supersedes two earlier ones and is the setting for the annual Cutlers' Feast. Enriching the banqueting hall are many fine portraits and tablets recording the names of some three hundred Master Cutlers, holders of the highest office in the leading guild of its kind in the world.

The Feast may be even older than the Company of Cutlers itself,

Roche Abbey, in the industrial district around Rotherham.

for it probably began as a continuation of a venison feast organised at an earlier time by the Earl of Shrewsbury. The present-day banquets are splendid affairs, colourful occasions surrounded by pomp and ceremony, and attended by such high-ranking personages as Cabinet Ministers and Ambassadors.

At Sheffield the Don loops northward to reach Rotherham, another place with an old chapel on a bridge. Built nearly five hundred years ago for the same purpose as the one at Wakefield, it too has been put to secular uses during its long lifetime, having been an almshouse, a jail, and a shop.

Like its Wakefield counterpart, it was threatened with demolition when the narrow width caused traffic jams. This menace occurred long before the advent of motor transport, and the bridge itself was widened in 1805. Happily the chapel was spared at that time, and it was preserved again when a new bridge was erected alongside to accommodate present-day traffic.

The splendid but blackened parish church at Rotherham reached its thousandth anniversary in 1937. It owes much to Primate Thomas, Archbishop of York, who held that exalted office from 1480 to 1501. A big benefactor of Rotherham, he made the parish church an ecclesiastic college, and was generous to the town in various other ways, never forgetting that it was his birthplace.

Henry VIII had the college suppressed and its buildings razed, but a doorway from it has been constructed in Boston Park, with stones salvaged from the ruins.

One of Yorkshire's most stately homes, Wentworth Woodhouse, stands in the alluring wooded park barely four miles from the middle of Rotherham. In one respect it outclasses all other great country seats in Britain. This ornate pile, which has been described as a palace rather than a mansion, is not just one house but *two*!

It gets its name from Thomas Wentworth, first Marquis of Rockingham, and is an amalgamation of a magnificent Venetian-style residence on the west and a Palladian one on the east. They were undergoing construction simultaneously, but the western palace was completed in 1734, whereas the eastern wing was not finished until the 1770s. With the connecting section, the façade is 600 feet long, bigger than the frontage of any other English country house.

The present Earl Fitzwilliam lives in part of Wentworth Wood-house, while the rest has become a training college for teachers, and there is no public access. Paths may be followed through the park, where there are two monuments of considerable interest, the Hoober Stand and Keppel's Column.

The Stand rises to a height of 100 feet, and terminates in a railed platform from which the towers and spires of fifty churches can be seen on a clear day. It was not built primarily as a view-tower, but was erected to commemorate the crushing of the '45 Rebellion.

Keppel's Column is a reminder of a court martial at which Admiral Keppel was accused of failing in his duties by letting the French Fleet escape after the Battle of Ushant in 1778.

He was acquitted, but his close friend the Marquis of Rockingham considered that the Admiral had been made to go through the court ordeal by corrupt politicans. Their aim was to make him a scapegoat for the unexpected result of the Ushant clash, rather than to admit that they were to blame for denying him enough money for the repair of his ships.

In addition to the pyramidal Hoober Stand, there is a second structure of that shape in the park. Known as the Needle's Eye, it is pierced by an arch. An unattested story says that this opening was used by a coachman to prove his skill. He boasted that he could drive a coach and pair through it, although the width of the vehicle allowed only a few inches at either side.

The pyramid, built specially for the test, was allowed to remain as a memorial after the unnamed whip had accomplished the feat.

The existence of two churches in one churchyard is not quite the rarity it is sometimes stated to be. In this respect, however, Wentworth Church, near Wentworth Woodhouse, transcends Heptonstall Church, Calderdale, described in Chapter I. Unlike other examples in different parts of the country, too, the older church is not entirely ruinous and disused. The chancel and north chapel are roofed and intact, and in 1925 the seventh Earl Fitzwilliam had them restored.

This temple is the ancient worshipping place of the family of Wentworth, many of them lying there. There are monuments to others of that distinguished line who are buried elsewhere—including Thomas Wentworth, first Earl of Strafford, who was beheaded on Tower Hill in 1641 after a travesty of a trial for treachery, though the whereabouts of his remains are now uncertain.

The supposition is that the earl's body was removed secretly from the Tower of London after his beheading and that it was brought to Hooton Roberts by his widow.

The first church on the site is thought to have been built in the years around 1235. Substantial alterations were made during the fifteenth, sixteenth and seventeenth centuries. There is evidence that some of the stones preserved in a vestry today were originally part of the Monk Bretton Priory, near Barnsley, and a built up archway in the north aisle came from the same source. The transfer was made in accordance with the will of a Thomas Wentworth who died in 1548 at the age of seventy.

The Don hereabouts runs through a ravine, dominated by two hills, one bearing Conisborough Castle, and the other surmounted by Conisborough Church. The surviving part of the fortress is the keep, put up on a man-made mound, by the powerful William de Warrenne, a favourite of William the Conqueror. The tower is almost cylindrical, and measures 52 feet across.

Tradition says that Hengist, brother of Horsa, who together led the first Saxons to reach England, was slain here. It goes on to say that a mound near the castle walls is his burial place.

You may be told that Warmsworth Church, midway between Conisborough and Doncaster, is the longest church in the country. It must certainly hold that record if there is any truth in the statement that it is nearly one mile in length!

Conisborough Castle, near Rotherham.

It is a trick claim, of course, which arises from the fact that the detached belfry is approximately a mile from the rest of the building. The bell tower is eight hundred years old, and a sixteen bell peal was rung in connection with a Norman church near the old hall and village. Nowadays it continues to summon the inhabitants of a new village a mile away to worship in their own church.

This is one of the churches in which John Wesley was permitted to preach. He was entertained at Wentworth Woodhouse, and the Marquis disturbed some friends by supporting the leader of what has since become known as Methodism.

The new church in the vicinity is a place of rare charm, designed in medieval style by J. L. Pearson, architect of many public buildings and churches, including Truro Cathedral.

The building began in 1873 and four years passed before the consecration was solemnised by the Archbishop of York. The central tower carries a splendid spire soaring to nearly 200 feet and there is seating for over five hundred people, including accommodation for children in an unusual series of specially designed pews.

The second Earl of Strafford gave various items of ecclesiastical plate to the old church in the 1660s, but the only one known to survive today is a hall-marked flagon of 1663.

Even the flagon was thought to have been purloined, but in 1894 it was found in a storeroom at Wentworth Woodhouse. The grime encrusting the object was carefully removed, revealing the true identity of this old church jug.

Was the executed Earl of Strafford buried in the old church at Wentworth? This was considered likely until 1895, when three skeletons, one decapitated, were dug up near the altar in Hooton Roberts church, between Rotherham and Doncaster, by workmen carrying out repairs. Covered with black velvet, the bones were obviously those of important persons, and the suggestion is that they were the remains of the tragic earl, his wife, and their daughter.

This successor to the old edifice was designed largely by a former rector. Another occupant of the rectory was the father of Francis Fawkes, the eighteenth century poet who wrote the words of the song 'The Brown Jug', but who was a gifted student of the Bible.

The church at Sprotborough is a treasure house of curiosities— carved bench-ends, hatchments, an alleged sanctuary chair, a one-handed clock face which is really a hoax, and symbols of trades and old traditions.

The pew ends include a pair skittishly illustrating 'before and after marriage', one being carved with two heads facing each other, and another with heads back to back. High on the wall is a rectangular adornment with a single pointer like that of a clock, but this does not tell the time. There is no mechanism, for this unusual object is in reality a unique style of hatchment, or funeral shield.

These shields bearing the coat-of-arms of a deceased person were hung outside the door of the house where they died, and were eventually placed in the church.

The ancestors of the Fitzwilliam family sprang from the Sprotborough neighbourhood, and in the Middle Ages it was a place important enough to have a regular market and market cross.

In bygone days the village was a temporary refuge for criminals as well as for the hungry. Wrongdoers could claim sanctuary in the church, and a relic there today is pointed out as a frith stool or sanctuary chair used in connection with the old custom.

Fugitives who succeeded in reaching such a chair were spared immediate retribution by their pursuers, but they were still liable to a judicial trial and banishment from the country if found guilty.

Some antiquarians, however, think that the so-called sanctuary chair at Sprotborough is nothing more exciting than the upper part of an old stone pulpit.

Just before Sprotborough the Don is joined by the Dearne, a stream rising about ten miles south-west of Wakefield and flowing past Barnsley and Darfield. Although most of the bridges spanning the Dearne nowadays are modern, ancient documents refer to one at Barnsley seven hundred years ago.

Barnsley is striving to cast off its reputation as a black and bleak town paying homage only to coal, and its appearance is being improved. The township has few historical treasures, and the parish church was rebuilt 1801–1802 (except for the five hundred years old tower), whilst the ambitious Town Hall dates only from the early 1930s. Despite its impressive appearance, according to Nikolas Pevsner, not all the money voted for the building has been spent well.

Of much greater antiquity are the ruins of Monk Bretton Priory, close to the Barnsley–Doncaster Road. The remains are not extensive and the chief relic is the arch of the gatehouse, but there are several reasons why the retreat merits attention. It is the only surviving example in Yorkshire of a Cluniac monastery, and it once figured in a long drawn out feud which involved Rome.

The Cluniacs were members of a 'break away' monastic Order, from the Benedictine priory at Pontefract. That establishment got much support from Adam Fitz-Swain, and he exercised his right as a big benefactor to control the 'alien' priory near Barnsley.

In course of time the Monk Bretton monks began to have doubts about the arrangement, claiming that they should have complete jurisdiction over their properties, having received many gifts which had made them rich. They were angry when Pontefract sent an unpopular monk to be the Prior of Monk Bretton.

The bitter quarrel caused the Cluniacs to despatch a deputation to the mother abbey at Cluny in France, asking for a decision about the dispute. The representatives from Yorkshire got no sympathy or support. On the contrary, they were abused and imprisoned. Another deputation, however, went to Rome and was rather more successful.

The complaint was considered by arbitrators who ruled that the monks of Monk Bretton should have the power to elect their Prior without interference, but his installation should be conducted by the Prior of Pontefract. Token payments should be paid to Pontefract in place of the higher amounts so far being remitted, and subjection money should also continue.

When the dissolution of our monasteries occurred at the behest of Henry VIII, the buildings which formed Monk Bretton Priory suffered. The ruins were converted into farm buildings, or were merely allowed to crumble. Part of the western range was converted into a residence in the late seventeenth century, but during the last fifty years much has been done by the Office of Works, as it was then called, to reveal the plan of the church and monastic buildings.

So on to Doncaster, which boasts a classic horserace, and which was the birthplace of a famous locomotive, and possesses one of the most important church organs in the country.

The annual turf race, the St. Leger, does not derive its name from any ecclesiastical source, despite appearances. It is named after Colonel St. Leger, who lived near Doncaster two hundred years ago. A keen racegoer, he initiated a sweepstake of 25 guineas each for three-year-olds, to be run over two miles at Doncaster in September 1776.

Turf historians, however, pinpoint the beginnings of the St. Leger as having really occurred two years later, when a dinner party took place at the Red Lion Inn, Doncaster. That gathering of horse-racing personalities was, indeed, the first time when the event received its now familiar name.

Without the intervention of the Marquis of Rockingham it would have come through turf history as the 'Rockingham Stakes', but he generously declined to sanction that title, stating that the idea for such a race was first mentioned to him by Colonel St. Leger.

Not only was that event the first official St. Leger, but it marked its introduction to Doncaster Town Moor. These facts put the Yorkshire race ahead of the 'Oaks' and the 'Derby' so far as age is concerned.

The lure of the St. Leger, which attracts a multitude each September, is so widely recognised that a hundred years ago the race was listed among the three most outstanding sights to be seen in Yorkshire. The other two were York Minster, and Sir Tatton Sykes of Sledmere.

Another creation of Doncaster origin, the *Flying Scotsman*, has toured the U.S.A. as well as Britain. Doncaster has continued to watch the widely varied career of this railway engine since it was built in the town's railway workshops during the early 1920s. The engine made railroad history by being the first locomotive to attain a speed of 100 m.p.h., a feat achieved in 1934. Doncaster engineers took pride in her efforts to hold this record until the *Mallard* bettered it to become the fastest engine operated by British Rail.

The ups and downs of the *Flying Scotsman* have nowhere been followed more closely during recent decades than in Doncaster. The news that it was to be scrapped, announced in 1963, was particularly painful there. The information that it was being saved from the scrapyard by a private benefactor rekindled interest in her future, and when it was put on show in spotless green and gold livery there were hopes that it was beginning a second life as a tourist attraction.

Officially known as L.N.E.R. locomotive No. 4472, this beloved giant of the railway tracks emigrated to America in 1969 with the hope that she might be adopted as a showpiece for railway enthusiasts in that part of the world. The scheme was unsuccessful, and the train was saved a second time only by the generosity of a second benefactor. He put up the money needed to bring the engine back to Britain, though it was then chartered by the Dart Valley

Light Railway to haul holidaymakers from Paignton to Kingswear and back again at not more than 25 m.p.h.

Yet the wince which this indignity probably caused in Doncaster may turn to smiles. The old flier is now pursuing its former enviable career by arrangements to re-introduce her to the British Rail track complex, for family runs and railways Fans' trips.

The *Flying Scotsman*'s shrill whistle as it tears along will be music to many ears, just as the notes of Doncaster's famous organ arouses musicians. The instrument was designed and built by Edmund Schulze, of Paulinzelle, who installed it in 1862. It was claimed at that time to be the biggest church organ in the country. At one period it was played by Wilfrid Sanderson, composer of 'Friend o' Mine', 'Drake Goes West', 'Until', and other well-known songs. He was organist at Doncaster Parish church from 1907 until 1924, after being tutored by Sir Frederick Bridge.

Edward Miller, a stonemason's son, who became a noted composer in the eighteenth century, served at Doncaster too, though this was before Schulze's lifetime. Miller's most widely used composition is the hymn tune 'Rockingham' for 'When I survey the Wondrous Cross'.

Despite its great historic importance, and its close associations with leading organists, the Schulze instrument at Doncaster has been played by other musicians who would not deny their much smaller ability. When it fell into disrepair a few years ago, the keyboards were made available to organists in general, and they were permitted to play it for five minutes at a charge of ten shillings. The money raised this way went towards the £2,500 needed to renovate the organ.

The pleasant low-lying village of Arksey, on the west bank of the Don beyond Doncaster, was once the property of Sir John Falstaff, the same burly knight made famous by Shakespeare. It came to Falstaff as a result of his marriage to a daughter of the family who had owned it previously, the Tibetots. They had received the estates by a grant from Edward I, but the male line became extinct in Falstaff's lifetime, and there were no serious obstacles to prevent his occupation of the area.

The village, though close to collieries, has managed to preserve its rustic appearance among lush meadows. It possesses a venerable church containing a font cover dated 1662, and the pulpit has stood since 1634. The church plate includes a cup and cover made in 1683 in London.

Nearby almshouses, and a school, help to make Arksey a delectable oasis in the surrounding mining area.

It is said that the ebullient Falstaff tried one of his little tricks here by selling his interests in the estates to two separate parties at the same time.

Fishlake, another warm-hued village of old world aspect, was originally just what its name suggests, an expanse of water stocked with fish. Close by is a church founded in Norman days.

Reclamation of the marshes was begun three hundred years ago by Cornelius Vermuyden, the Dutch civil engineer whose name crops up at various other places immediately south of the Ouse in connection with similar schemes, though the one at Fishlake was not completed until after his death.

The most valued part of the church fabric is its Norman arch over the south entrance. Now sheltered by a modern porch, the arch is carved with representations of both real and imaginary creatures, a monk in a boat, knights jousting, dragons fighting, men carrying a coffin, a griffin, and a canopied figure holding a staff of office. The door itself was originally at Roche Abbey, east of Rotherham.

William Rokeby, Archbishop of Dublin and Lord Chancellor of Ireland in the sixteenth century, was born at Kirk Sandal, the Don-side village which stands on the bylane route from Rotherham to Thorne. He was rector here before being elevated to higher offices, and the church he served owes its peculiar appearance partly to his incumbency.

A chapel added to the edifice as a memorial to him is bigger than the chancel. Another oddity is that the nave and aisles are wider than they are long. The porch tower with its pyramid roof has been described by one authority as 'ridiculous'.

Archbishop Rokeby, who died in 1521, has a monument against the north wall. If the instructions in his will were duly observed, however, his heart was removed and interred at Halifax.

The nearby market town of Thorne is another place where the genius of Dutch civil engineers was exercised some three hundred years ago. Huguenots and other refugees also helped to drain the surrounding area, and the Don reaches Goole by way of a four mile artificial waterway called the Dutch Canal.

CHAPTER V

Wharfedale

Each of the Yorkshire dales has its own character and presents itself in individual ways. Wharfedale is no exception to this general rule, and with the possible exclusion of Wensleydale, is the most attractive river valley in the county.

Rising near Cam Fell, the mountain ridge a few miles from the Yorkshire–Westmorland border, the Wharfe provides an ideal combination of water, woods, crags, high fells, windswept moors, subterranean marvels, bridges, monastic remains, and old castles. Scenically it ranges from quiet pastoral stretches to sylvan surroundings and the heather covered territories of curlew and grouse.

It embraces all these attractions during its journey to join the Ouse near Cawood—a distance of seventy-five miles, making it Yorkshire's third longest river. Yet this usually delightful dale has sometimes exhibited a more sinister nature, being the scene of raging floods and overthrown bridges.

On one occasion the overflowing Wharfe carried live fish into the nave of Hubberholme Church. Happily, this picturesque building from the early thirteenth century has withstood the onslaught of other elements and today is a remarkable treasury of ecclesiastical souvenirs.

The most important is the oaken rood-loft, which in bygone days supported a rood or crucifix, which was fashioned by a craftsman called William Jaker in 1558. Singers also occupied this exalted position, and the Gospels were read from it when high mass was celebrated.

The loft is the only one surviving in the West Riding now and there is only a single further example, at Flamborough, in the whole county.

A bell from 1601 is cherished here, though it is no longer rung but displayed as a showpiece. One of the two altars has had a checkered history. It was put aside when the other was introduced,

Buckden, Wharfedale.

and the landlord of the nearby George Inn coveted the object so much that he had it removed to the hostelry for use as an ale bench. He claimed that he was entitled to put the altar to any purpose he wished, because he was also the parish clerk.

Eventually this secular usage was disallowed, and the altar was returned to the church. Its companion there was originally at University College, Oxford.

Church and inn have other affinities. The inn was the vicarage long ago, and for many years was the setting for a strange land-letting ceremony—a kind of auction timed by candlelight, the last bid before the flame flickered out being the rent payable for a plot of land owned by the church.

The money is earmarked for distribution among the poor in the neighbourhood, but in recent years there have been very few applicants for such help, although between £60 and £70 has been available.

Until 1971 the vicar acted as go-between for the bidders, but in that year the ceremony was brought more up to date, a Skipton auctioneer having been engaged to conduct the sale. Sticklers for the retention of our old customs may find the lapse of this ancient style of auction at Hubberholme rather disturbing.

Downstream from this quiet spot is Buckden, once the headquarters of foresters whose job was to protect the surrounding area as a feudal chase. The name of the village means the valley of bucks, and a herd of these lovely animals grazed here until twenty years ago, continuing a custom begun in Norman times and long administered by the Percys of Northumberland.

The bridge at Buckden was of considerable importance in the era of packhorse transport, being used by ponies to carry lead ore from nearby mines to smelting mills, or taking wool from flocks of sheep grazed on the fells. Two hundred years ago, when this bridge was only half its present width, it was known locally as Election Bridge. The nickname arose from a speech made by a would-be Member of Parliament, in which he promised to have a new bridge built if the villagers would cast their votes in his favour. This they did, but to keep faith it was necessary to use funds really provided for the repair of Hubberholme Bridge.

There used to be regular markets at Kettlewell, three miles downstream from Buckden, and in those days Ketil, as it was called in honour of a Norse settler, was the capital of this part of Wharfedale. It still retains its market place although traders no longer congregate there and the fairs which were once a big attraction have lapsed.

General view of Buckden, Wharfedale.

View over Wharfedale to Kettlewell.

The road up Littondale, from near Hawkswick.

The village is an airy, clean spot, much frequented by motorists, and has three substantial inns for their use. The present church only dates back to 1820, but it replaces a Norman one, and in medieval days a considerable amount of property hereabouts was owned by the monastic houses of Bolton, Fountains, and Coverham, as well as the baronial Nevilles and other high-ranking families.

Some twentieth century fame has come to Kettlewell, for it was the home of the author C. J. Cutcliffe Hyne. He lies in the church-yard, his resting place marked by a boulder from the fells he loved, and the name of the village lives on in the character of 'Captain Kettle', the best-known character in his books.

The River Skirfare, which flows through lovely Littondale to join the Wharfe between Kettlewell and Kilnsey, is the delight of fishermen, though in bygone days its leading ambassador was The Wise Woman of Littondale. A popular fortuneteller, she travelled regularly from her hovel in Arncliffe to Skipton, where her demonstrations of soothsaying proved profitable.

Only a short distance down the dale from the confluence of the Skirfare and the Wharfe is the natural wonder, Kilnsey Crag, the

170 feet high immense cliff of outcropping limestone overhanging its base by 40 feet.

On to Grassington, the metropolis of this part of the Dale. Now largely a pleasure resort and a place for retirement, it was formerly an important centre for lead-mining. Many of the old shafts and other workings can be found on the neighbouring fells.

Strangely, the town has no Anglican church of its own, the one at Linton across the Wharfe serving for both places. Nevertheless, Grassington does not lack buildings of historical importance. The Old Hall, at the foot of the main road to the west, is one of the oldest domestic structures in Yorkshire.

Incorporating thirteenth century features, it still has a medieval appearance and, unlike many other old houses, it is not just a show-place, but has been occupied in our day. Some of the windows date from Tudor times, while others are seven hundred years old. Small dwellings of this age, as distinct from castles, are extremely rare throughout Britain, especially examples tenanted until recent decades.

Grassington Old Hall was built by the Plumptons of Nessfield, near Ilkley, one of the lesser families who shared in the partitioning of England by William of Normandy. A descendant lost his estates for siding with the barons who rebelled against King John, but was given back his properties soon after the monarch's death.

The old residence at Grassington then reverted to its role as a tenement for a forester and his staff who guarded the surrounding area against poachers.

Linton, as already stated, provides for Grassington church-goers. The Reverend Benjamin Smith, an eccentric pastor here, thought more about dancing than pastoral duties. He often forsook his flock to visit the Old Assembly Rooms in Leeds, where he was prominent among the dancers.

A curiosity about the long, low church is that, whilst it occupies a riverside site, it is dedicated to St. Michael. Such churches almost invariably stand on hills, and there is no apparent reason why this saint's name should be applied to the low-lying one at Linton.

The hamlet is not one to be passed by swiftly. Overlooking the green are imposing almshouses founded in the eighteenth century by a somewhat mysterious benefactor who made a fortune in London, but whose ties with Linton are obscure. The retreat was enlarged a century later, and the apartments were given up-to-date

Kilnsey Crag.

amenities a few years ago, without destroying their old-world appearance.

Equally worth observing is the nearby humpbacked bridge spanning Linton Beck, a tributary of the Wharfe. The structure has wide inviting approaches, but narrows to less than 4 feet at the centre.

The old bridge was frequently under water, preventing Linton people from reaching the church on the other side.

Two local sisters therefore opened a fund to pay for an arched bridge, as this type would be less subject to flooding. Local farmers, however, failed to subscribe, putting forward various paltry excuses for refusing financial help, and smiling when the sisters announced that the new bridge would be put up at their own expense.

The farmers' delight turned to chagrin when they realised that the benefactresses had outwitted them. The bridge was wide at the entrance, but narrowed so greatly at the middle that only pedestrians could get across. Farm vehicles could not be driven over the structure, as they had expected. As a result of their meanness, they had to use the adjoining ford and accept the risks of the Linton Beck at times of flood.

The man who founded the Linton almshouses was by no means the only large-scale benefactor to Wharfedale. Burnsall had its own 'Dick Whittington', William Craven, who was born at Appletreewick close by, and made the journey to London in search of fame and fortune in the seventeenth century.

He achieved both, first being knighted when he became rich as a merchant, and later receiving an earldom. Like the famous Dick, he was also made Mayor, the office of *Lord* Mayor not existing in his time, but he did not forget his Yorkshire origins.

He paid for improvements to the route from Appletreewick to Burnsall Church, restored that place of worship at his personal expense, and founded Burnsall Grammar School. It is still an attractive feature of the village, and continues in use.

Barden, three miles down the Dale, has memories of another benefactor, Lady Anne Clifford, of Skipton, who restored Barden Tower, the eye-catching former hunting lodge of her family.

When Lady Anne first saw the building in the mid-seventeenth century, it was in a decrepit state. But, as an inscription over the entrance records, she had it made habitable again. Its present ruinous condition is not due to any neglect on her part, but it fell

Burnsall, the old Grammar School.

into ruin after thieves had stripped lead from the roof less than two hundred years ago.

Notice the ancient church nearby. It is no longer used for services. For many years the keeper living in the adjoining cottage was also the bellringer, and it is said that one such tenant had the bellrope diverted into the tiny house so that he could ring the bell without getting out of bed.

The misnamed Bolton Abbey (it was really a Priory) was occupied by Augustinian canons who did not confine themselves to a cloistered life. Their duties took them far afield to conduct services in parish churches and carry out other parochial work.

The first band to reach Wharfedale came from Embsay, near Skipton, where they had tried to establish a priory. They found the site too remote and bleak, although the original canons struggled there for thirty years. Their privations were brought to the notice of Alicia, daughter of Robert de Romille, a Norman who overran the Skipton area after 1066.

Alicia allowed the canons to seek a better spot, and in 1154 she signed a document enabling them to start building a new priory at Bolton, Wharfedale, on land which she endowed.

The building was in almost continual expansion until it was confiscated by Henry VIII in 1542. Indeed, a second western tower similar to the one on the present church was begun only twenty years or so before the Dissolution. Nor was the entire priory made ruinous. The nave was preserved for use as the parish church, and has that role today. There has been no break in the continuity from the twelfth century.

Apart from its associations with the Augustinian Order, the Priory as it stands today has mementoes of comparatively recent events, including a reminder of an assassination which shocked the nation in the early 1880s.

An ornately carved cross, modelled after the Runic ones found in various localities, stands in the burial ground on the north-western side of the ruins. It was set up at the expense of the tenants of the surrounding ducal estate, and is in memory of Lord Frederick Cavendish, son of the seventh Duke of Devonshire, murdered in Phoenix Park, Dublin, on 6th May 1882.

Lord Frederick had arrived in Ireland only twelve hours earlier to become Chief Secretary to Earl Spencer, Lord-Lieutenant of Ireland. Out walking with Thomas Henry Burke, both he and his companion were set upon by a gang of political extremists, and Lord Frederick was fatally stabbed.

The rectory near the Priory bears the badge of the Boyles, the family name of the Earls of Cork and Burlington. The house, however, was once the village school. Under a charitable trust founded in 1700, the local inhabitants were given the choice of having either a school or an almshouse, and they opted for a school. The premises remained in educational use until a new school was opened at Beamsley in 1874. The old school then became the rectory for the minister in charge of Bolton Priory parish church.

Beamsley's place in Wharfedale history centres mostly round the almshouses alongside the road to Harrogate. The archway leading to the series of small apartments bears the Clifford coat of arms, which are re-emblazoned from time to time, and alongside the badge is a tablet pointing out that this retreat was founded in Elizabethan days by the Countess of Cumberland, and more richly endowed by her daughter, the bountiful Lady Anne Clifford, whose beneficence we have already noted in connection with Barden Tower, and who generously restored Skipton Parish Church after it was damaged during the Civil Wars.

Turning back to Bolton Bridge, the Wharfe continues to Ilkley, where it is spanned by two bridges, one old and the other modern. The ancient humpbacked structure, now closed to vehicles, replaces at least two earlier ones swept away by raging torrents. The bridge standing now dates from about the mid-1670s, its immediate forerunner having been 'overturned' in 1673 by a flood which also demolished Barden Bridge and devastated other parts of Wharfedale.

However, compared with other aspects of Ilkley's history, that disaster was a modern occurrence. No other place in Yorkshire embraces such a long stretch of time as do the relics to be seen in and around this resort. It became a spa in 1843, yet it was known for its waters from the Roman Occupation.

The legions from Rome, who had a military and trading station at Ilkley (they called it Olicana) may have channelled the moorland stream which fills two baths at White Wells, the building looking down on the present town. This bath-house was not erected until the eighteenth century and fell into disuse only recently. A business-man has latterly been given permission to convert it into an exhibition gallery and a warden's house, and there are hopes that

The old bridge, Ilkley.

archaeological studies on the site will provide evidence of Roman interest there.

Even the Roman era is made insignificant in historical chronology by the knowledge that the jungle which clothed the slopes of the valley in primeval days was occupied by some early people. Traces of their existence and culture are in the form of cup-and-ring carvings on rocks in the Ilkley vicinity.

Still more startling is the fact that the symbol incised on one big boulder has also been found in European countries and even in the Far East. It is a loop design known as a swastika, but just who carved it, and when they did so, are mysteries yet to be conclusively solved.

The Saxon period is represented by three crosses in the parish churchyard. They came to light last century, one doing duty as a gatepost. They are over thirteen hundred years old, and the central one is the most complete, although the head cross is missing. The symbols on the stonework are not easily identified, but they include the emblems of the four evangelists and a number of animal figures. The shaft nearest to the church porch apparently served as a preaching cross, for it carries a representation of a cleric wearing robes, and it also shows a scroll.

Rombald's Moor, as the breezy area separating Wharfedale from Airedale is sometimes named on maps, is not the heath it used to be, the grass and other botanical growths having been eroded to bare rock and compacted soil. The first step towards the restoration, however, has already been taken by enlisting the help of ramblers to survey the region and suggest ways in which they would like it to be landscaped.

One strange feature is Cowper's Cross, a monument near the rough track over the Moor to Keighley. Its singularity is that nobody knows why it stands there. The popular tradition that it marks the grave of a wayfarer who perished in a blizzard has no written confirmation.

The name of the relic suggests that it is an old market cross, *Cowper* or *cooper* being the old term for an itinerant trader. Yet plainly no market can ever have been held on this exposed and isolated spot. So, if it *is* a market cross, it must have once stood elsewhere.

A close examination of the relic has not drawn attention to any markings. Nevertheless the Calvary Cross on top of the pillar has been shown to be out of place. It includes a yard-long section which was once part of the main shaft. This part evidently broke off at some date now unknown and was used to repair the cross head when that broke too, and a section was lost.

Two modern crosses, modelled after the Runic ones preserved in Ilkley parish churchyard, enhance the main road at Burley-in-Wharfedale on the way to Otley. One is in memory of W. E. Forster, the Member of Parliament who, a century ago piloted through parliament the bill for free education. Born in Dorset, he considered Burley as his home, and represented Bradford in the Commons continuously for twenty-five years.

His family were Quakers and he abhored using force to check violence. When he was sent to Dublin as Secretary for Ireland, political troubles there necessitated the use of guns, but he substituted lead shot for bullets.

After initial financial difficulties, he became a rich mill-owner, and championed factory workers and their rights, associating with other supporters of their cause, such as Robert Owen and Thomas Cooper.

The other memorial at Burley honours Forster's close friend and business associate William Fison, who established a textile factory in the village, running the machinery by harnessing the River Wharfe.

Thomas Chippendale's genius has been commemorated only belatedly at Otley, for not until the last few years has the town publicised the fact that the famous cabinetmaker was a native of the place. A tablet now marks the site of the cottage where he was born, there are Chippendale chairs in the council chamber, and a society for those interested in him, and his life-story flourishes.

Some of his most cherished work in Wharfedale is at Harewood House. On the way there from Otley is Arthington's Nunnery House, a singular home because of the large number of panes in the windows. The total exceeds three hundred, but many of the tiny 'eyes', as they might be called, are blind, being without glass. The panes were replaced with slate slabs nearly three hundred years ago, when William III taxed windows to meet a coinage deficiency. The levy forced many owners of large houses to block up every window they could spare.

Officially the many-windowed property at Arthington is called Nunnery House. It takes the name from a Cluniac retreat founded

Nunnery House, Arthington.

on or near the same site in 1150. The nunnery continued until it was suppressed in 1540. Parts of the masonry were used in erecting the present domestic dwelling, which was begun in 1585.

Harewood Castle, glimpsed from Harewood Bank on the Otley–Wetherby road, is not to be confused with Harewood House, the seat of the Earl of Harewood. The two buildings are in the same extensive parkland, yet the castle was erected centuries before the mansion.

The fortress, now only a shell, had its heydays five to six hundred years ago, having been built about 1367 by Sir William Aldburgh in a form rare at that period. He avoided the old Norman conception of a plain fortified house, introducing elaborations, instead of adopting the austerity common to castles in the fourteenth century. Even after the passing of hundreds of years the pile is imposing and some of the ornamentations repay a careful inspection.

The main entrance bears the armorial crest of the founder, together with the family motto, 'What shall be, shall', and more heraldry enhances a small chamber believed to have been an oratory. High up in an interior wall is a decorated fireplace, the seemingly odd position being explained by the disappearance of the

Harewood Castle.

floor, and on the west side of the great hall is a canopied recess similar to a tomb.

Sir William Aldburgh was an officer in the court of Edward Balliol, King of Scotland, and the badge of the Scottish monarch appears on the castle as well as the Aldburgh coat-of-arms.

The alliance between the Yorkshire knight and Balliol was so strong that the Scottish sovereign fled to Harewood and took refuge there when he had to renounce his crown.

This historic pile became uninhabitable sometime between 1630 and 1641, but the reason is now unknown. The stronghold is the remains of one of three great houses built at Harewood, the second being Gawthorpe Hall, which stood on the present lake. Harewood village was also close to the hall, but it was moved to its present position on the Leeds–Harrogate road to make way for the Harewood House of today, so that the occupants of this stately home could have privacy.

That attribute has been much impaired in recent years by the opening of Harewood House and gardens to the public. One of the most popular 'open houses' in Britain, it was built two hundred years ago, a fine achievement and an example of close collaboration between the leading architects, decorators, and cabinet-makers of the time—John Carr, Robert Adam, Thomas Chippendale, Joseph Ross, Angelica Kauffmann, Antonio Zucchi, and others.

Long before it became the home of Princess Mary and the sixth Earl of Harewood, this impressive residence saw royalty in its splendid apartments. The Tsar of Russia was entertained there in 1816, Queen Victoria came in 1835, and the Queen Dowager, Adelaide, wife of William IV, was a guest in 1830.

Today the apartments are treasure stores of antique furniture, priceless chinaware, immensely valuable paintings, and a variety of other possessions collected by successive Earls. The gardens and lake attract thousands of tourists, and an aviary with rare birds is a mecca for ornithologists.

Harewood Avenue, more than a mile long, forms a bowery route to Collingham and Wetherby. One of the cherished souvenirs at Collingham is church property—a rare cresset stone with eight hollows in which oil and floating wicks used to light the church.

Wetherby has catered for travellers for a long time, first by accommodating coach passengers and later developing services for motor vehicles. The town is on the Great North Road and some of the inns used to stable stagecoach horses, ready to take over from sweating animals which had drawn the cumbrous carriages along stages to the north or south.

A double line of lime trees marks the approach to Newton Kyme hall and church, between Wetherby and Tadcaster. Yet there are no gates guarding this avenue. The approach was gated until the reign of Charles II, but open access was then demanded as a penalty for help given to Roundheads by the Fairfaxes living at the hall, and the gates were removed.

The family, whose properties spread also to Menston and Denton, in other parts of Wharfedale, provided history with a number of illustrious characters. Newton Kyme Hall was the birthplace of Admiral Robert Fairfax, a scion who ran away from his tutor and sailed from Whitby when he was only fifteen.

Gaining rapid promotion he distinguished himself by helping Admiral Byng to capture Gibraltar in 1704. He took part in the

Harewood House—south front and terraces.

battle of Malaga and shared the siege of Barcelona with Sir Cloudesley Shovel.

Yet he never lost his love for the countryside of Yorkshire, and on retiring from the Royal Navy he settled down in the Fairfax mansion at Newton Kyme.

The hall we see today is mostly in the form he ordained, and he also had a second avenue planted across the estate, using trees from Denton Park, near Ilkley.

He lies in the venerable church near the great house at Newton Kyme, and his monument there bears a carving of one of the ships he commanded, recalling his naval career.

A more widely celebrated figure connected with this rural church was no less than John Milton, the poet, who once read the lessons here.

The altar plate includes a chalice believed to have belonged to Owen Oglethorpe, the Bishop of Carlisle, who crowned Elizabeth I, after other high dignitaries of the church had declined to do so. The chalice was left behind at Newton Kyme rectory, where arrangements for the coronation were discussed.

Residents of Tadcaster can justifiably claim that their town 'goes back to the Ark', for a timber-framed building in Kirkgate has long been referred to as 'The Ark' because two carvings of human heads on the corbels are reputed to represent Noah and his wife.

The property is really no more than a wing of a bigger two-bay hall erected during the second half of the fifteenth century, and is the oldest house in the town today. At one period it served as an inn called the Falcon, one of no less than twenty-four inns in Tadcaster at the height of the coaching era, when fifty coaches travelled through each day between York and Leeds alone.

The inn is thought to have derived its name from the Falcon appearing on the Yorkist badge during the Wars of the Roses.

As a dwelling house the building originally consisted of just one room, and there was no fireplace, the fire being in the centre of the floor, with an escape hole in the roof for the smoke. That was in the late fifteenth and early sixteenth centuries, but more comfort was subsequently provided by adding an upper floor, fireplaces, and a chimney stack.

The Ark was occupied until the mid 1950s, serving as a staff cottage for a local brewery. It has since reverted to a one-room house and is now a museum. The chimney stack has been removed, and an inside gallery has been erected so that visitors may get a good general impression of the kind of surroundings in which Tadcaster people lived five hundred years ago.

At one time the building was known as Morley Hall, because it was used as a Dissenters' preaching place when Robert Morley was prominent among people of that persuasion. There is even a belief in some quarters that representatives of the Pilgrim Fathers met here to discuss their plans to sail to the New World.

The tragedy of Cardinal Wolsey's downfall is inseparable from Cawood, the last place near the Wharfe before the river joins the Ouse. The illstarred cleric was arrested here in 1530, having displeased Henry VIII, and was escorted towards London, but died at Leicester, a broken man, unable to complete the journey.

Only scanty parts of Cawood Castle, the residence of a succession of archbishops of York, now survive. But the fifteenth century gatehouse through which Wolsey rode in disgrace is to be seen. It stands as a reminder that the stronghold here was for centuries the Windsor of the North (though Middleham Castle, in Uredale, also claims the title), serving as setting for royal courts and banquets unparalleled elsewhere in Britain.

When George Neville, brother of Warwick the Kingmaker, became Archbishop of York in 1465, he celebrated his appointment at Cawood by giving an immense feast which required 1,000 sheep, 500 deer, and 1,000 oxen. Some 2,000 cooks were needed to prepare the feast, which also included great numbers of game birds and large quantities of fish.

Begun in Saxon days by Athelstane, and made into a palace six hundred years ago, Cawood Castle ended its days of glory in 1644, when the Royalists were completely routed at Marston Moor and the victorious Roundheads ordered it to be dismantled.

The comparison with Windsor Castle arises from the long list of kings, queens, high church dignitaries, noble warriors, dazzling courtiers, and rich revellers who came to Cawood. Among them were Henry II and Queen Eleanor, Edward II, and Henry VIII and Catherine Howard.

It is a pity that, apart from the ornate gatehouse, so little of the palatial building has survived, but its destruction cannot remove the historic atmosphere of the site.

In the eleventh century a Benedictine monk from France occupied a cell on a bank of the Ouse barely four miles south of Cawood. The advantages of the site are said to have been revealed to him in a dream, and here he built a small wooden church with a cross visible from the river.

It was spotted by Hugh de Lacy, High Sheriff of Yorkshire, who drew the attention of William the Conqueror to the Monk's devotions. William granted rich lands to endow and extend the tiny church along monastic lines, and this was the beginning of Selby Abbey. The monk was the first of more than thirty successive abbots, and part of the original Benedictine church still forms part of the Abbey Church.

The great edifice has undergone various vicissitudes, including the collapse of its central tower in 1690 and a disastrous fire which gutted most of the interior in 1906. Restorations have since made the edifice one of the most magnificent abbeys in the land.

CHAPTER VI

Nidd, Ure, and Wensleydale

From pastoral scenery to semi-Alpine grandeur—that's a simple description of Nidderdale, the valley of the stream which has its origin amid the wild moors east of Whernside and unites with the Ouse about six miles from York. Its nearest companion, the Ure, is commonly regarded as the major contributory to the great waterway finally forming the Humber, though the Swale adds a considerable quota beyond Boroughbridge.

The Nidd valley has a host of interests for tourists and visitors. Among its attractions are the delightful market town of Knaresborough, the spa and conference centre of Harrogate, Ripley, with its castle, the grotesque rocks on Brimham Moor, villages associated with such contrasting personalities as Guy Fawkes, and the composer of the 'Indian Love Lyrics', and large man-made lakes enhancing the natural landscape.

At the head of the dale are the Angram and Scar House reservoirs created by Bradford Corporation as feeders for the two mile long Gowthwaite reservoir farther downstream. Deadman's Hill, on the high land above the first named enclosure of water, gets its name from a horrible triple murder recorded in the registers of Middlesmoor.

Three decapitated bodies were found there in 1728, and were assumed to be the mortal remains of three Scots pedlars murdered by robbers, though another account states that they were lured to a farmhouse, and their heads severed to prevent identification before the bodies were buried well away from the scenes of the crime.

Whatever the exact circumstances may have been, the perpetration of such a murder is undeniable. The Middlesmoor registers record the payment of fees to the coroner, the sexton, and other people concerned with the reinterment of 'three murder'd bodies found burrd on Ledge Edge without heads'.

In this locality of caves and 'swallow holes' the Nidd emulates the Aire in Malhamdale by going underground for two miles. Middlesmoor, despite its wild surroundings, is thought to have been visited by St. Chad, the seventh century Bishop of Lichfield and Primate of York. An unusual Saxon cross preserved here is believed to have been set up by this champion of Celtic Christianity.

More illustrious family connections surround Pateley Bridge, the gateway to Upper Nidderdale, the district having long been gener-ously served by the Yorkes. Their seat, Bewerley Hall, was razed in 1926, but a reminder of their benefactions is a mock ruin on the edge of the moors overlooking the town. It was built in the form of a crumbled abbey, in the days when landowners considered that such structures improved the view, and the construction of Yorke's Folley, as it was called, provided work for men in the area at a time of widespread unemployment.

The road to Ripley and Harrogate passes through Hampsthwaite, where the ancestors of W. M. Thackeray had their roots. An in-scription pointing out this fact is in the porch of the parish church, but the most striking memorial inside the building is a tomb bearing a marble figure of a reclining lady.

This monument commemorates Amy Woodforde-Finden, whose 'Indian Love Lyrics' are known all over the world, and who lived at Hampsthwaite at the time of her death in 1919. Scenes represent-ing her songs ornament the Yorkshire resting place of this gifted composer.

Oliver Cromwell spent an uncomfortable night at Ripley Castle, the seat of the Ingilbys since it was built more than four hundred years ago. He was reluctantly dined and wined in the great hall by Lady Ingilby after the Battle of Marston Moor. Her Royalist sym-pathies were impressed upon Cromwell by the pistols in her apron strings, while she acted as hostess to the general and his officers. She is reputed to have told him, as he left Ripley the next day, that if his men had failed to behave themselves he would not have left her house alive.

Now that the Ripon–Harrogate road by-passes Ripley, the village has reverted to the quiet life which motor traffic largely destroyed. The gatehouse of the Castle is part of an older stronghold, and a detour to see it, and to go sightseeing in the vicinity, is well worth-while. The mansion is open to the public on Sundays and Bank Holidays from June to September; on Saturdays the gardens may be visited.

The cobbled square in front of the gatehouse is complete with a fifteenth century market cross and stocks, and a spring nearby is adorned with a stone head of a boar, part of the Ingilby insignia.

The churchyard contains a rarity, the base of a weeping cross marking the end of a corpse road from higher up the dale. The cut-away parts have often been described as knee-holes for praying mourners but were in reality receptacles for votive offerings.

Probably the best known view of Nidderdale is the one obtained from the terraces and courtyard of Knaresborough Castle. From this vantage point just off the town centre a fascinating stretch of the winding river unfolds, with boats far below, cottages like dolls' houses lining the riverside walks, and the towering railway viaduct providing a series of arches which frame sections of the picture.

Were such a structure proposed today, its construction would most certainly be criticised by 'conservationists'. Yet this feature is now an integral part of Knaresborough and is regarded as an improvement to the view, and not an eyesore.

Charles I looked on the scene before it was altered, but he had little opportunity to admire it, for he was brought to Knaresborough on the way to London, and lodged in the Castle.

The fortress has witnessed many other dramatic events. Another monarch imprisoned there was Richard II, and the assassin of Thomas à Becket took refuge in it after fleeing from Canterbury. The stronghold owes its present ruinous condition to the Civil War.

At the foot of Water Bog Lane is a thatched dwelling which was originally used as a summer house for the nearby Manor House. In olden days the term 'summer house' meant a house for summer occupation, and not just a wooden retreat in a garden. Manor Cottage also served as a lodging house for priests visiting the Manor House.

The premises surrounding the market place include a shop claimed to be the oldest retail pharmaceutical business in the country. Old recipe books have been preserved, together with utensils used in preparing medicines. At one period dogs were employed in turning a grinding machine, a device for crushing ingredients.

In 1785 a mill for producing linen articles from flax grown and spun in Nidderdale was established on the river bank below Knaresborough Castle. Fine linen goods are still made there, and it is the oldest linen mill running in England today. Moreover the

Knaresborough Castle, Nidderdale.

owners possess one of the most remarkable garments ever made—a linen shirt woven in 1850 by a local master weaver named George Hemshall. Its singularity is that it has no seam or joint of any kind, though it has a collar and cuffs.

If a scheme put forward for the town last century had been carried out, Knaresborough would probably have lost much of its present charm. Sir Titus Salt sought to make it a manufacturing town, but his plan was vetoed by the local authorities. He went to the Shipley area instead, and built Saltaire Mills, together with the adjoining model estate for his workpeople.

The medicinal properties of Harrogate's springs were first pointed out by Captain William Slingsby in 1571. He pointed out the similarity between these waters and those of the spa at Saviniere, Germany.

The most astonishing feature of the Yorkshire town's healing springs, however, is their great variety. No fewer than thirty bubble up in a small part of the Valley Gardens, and they are all different in chemical content. The taking of the waters without payment was covered by clauses in the Act of Parliament which, in 1770, permitted the enclosing of Knaresborough Forest. It was also stipulated that there was to be no hindrance of people wishing to reach the wells.

The original spa building, the Pump Room, was not erected until 1842, though the old Sulphur Well, as it was called, had a protective dome before that date. When the Pump House was being built, the old circular open-sided pavilion was removed to another spring, known as Tewit Well, on the Stray. The future of this historic structure has several times been in jeopardy, but its restoration has been carried out as recently as 1973.

The Nidd skirts Cowthorpe before joining the Ouse near Nun Monkton, and the former village has two claims to attention. It has the remnants of the famous Cowthorpe Oak, alas! no longer alive, though for many generations it was the oldest living thing in Britain, having been a sapling at the time of the Roman Occupation. The nearby church once had Guy Fawkes as a bellringer. He made the long journey from his home at Scotton, near Knaresborough, to pull the bellrope at Cowthorpe.

The maypole on the green at Nun Monkton has been a subject of controversy. A pole of Russian pine was set up in 1878, but there was an older oaken one on the same spot, and the year when this earlier pole was erected has never been satisfactorily confirmed. The date most often mentioned in 1793.

Nun Monkton derives its name from the fact that a monk occupied a cell in the vicinity in Saxon days. The prefix refers to a Benedictine nunnery established close by in King Stephen's reign. The exquisite church, which one authority has described as one of the architectural treats of Yorkshire, contains an incised grave slab believed to have covered the sepulchre of a prioress who presided over the nunnery in the thirteenth century. The church as a whole was the priory chapel, but the village property known as The Priory is a residence built about 1690. It demonstrates the influence of Dutch immigrants who settled in this neighbourhood at that period.

Rising near Abbotside Common, and overlooked by the wild Great Shunner Fell, the Ure could be excused if it gave at least part of its allegiance to Cumbria, for it has its beginning almost on the borderline between that county and Yorkshire.

The river has barely set out on its course before it passes one of the most isolated churches in England. The tiny edifice caters for the sparsely populated area around Lunds. It became even more remote when a new road was constructed on the other bank of the Ure for traffic going to and from Kirkby Stephen, in Westmorland.

The first place of importance in Uredale is Hardraw, backed by its famous Scar with a waterfalll plunging more than 100 feet over a crag. The Gothic church owes much to the lordly Wharncliffe family, who used to hunt in the neighbourhood. Sedbusk is interesting for its 'mazeholes' or tunnels and caves.

On the other side of the river is Hawes, a grey market town with a church rebuilt in 1851, and restored since 1930, though there was a place of worship on a different site hereabouts in the fifteenth century.

Aysgarth Church was rebuilt, except for the tower, in 1866 but its interior contains cherished examples of medieval woodcarving. A 35 feet long screen which divided the chancel from the rest of the building until just over a century ago is considered to be one of the finest in Yorkshire. Parts of an ancient bench are set into the reading desk. They are decorated with carvings of a lion, an antelope, and the letter W with a tun and a hazel tree, these last named forming a pictorial name, that of William de Heslington, one-time Abbot of Jervaulx Abbey, between Middleham and Masham.

These various examples of the craft of woodcarving were probably executed by carvers from Ripon, and according to some investigators they came to Aysgarth not from Jervaulx but from Coverham Abbey, where they also provided much of the woodwork.

The natural attraction of Aysgarth is its spectacular series of waterfalls. At times of flood their roar can be heard from six miles away like thundering horses. The bridge which carries the main road through the dale, and divides the Upper Force from the Lower Force, was originally only 9 feet wide and dates from at least the sixteenth century, a local man having left money for its repair in 1594. The falls are not deeply plunging cascades but watersteps or terraces over which the Ure tumbles tempestuously, like a gigantic staircase.

Bainbridge, four miles from Hawes, gives Uredale a further link with Ripon. The village, clustering round a spacious green has a hornblowing ceremony like the one observed every evening at Ripon. At Bainbridge, however, the blasts are not blown throughout the year, but only during winter. They were originally intended to guide benighted travellers through the nearby forests.

The section of the valley known as Wensleydale uses Aysgarth

Aysgarth Falls. The vicinity is renowned for its beautiful natural cascades.

Bainbridge, Wensleydale.

as its western gateway and continues to the village of Wensley at the eastern end, with the romantic Bolton Castle clearly seen beyond Redmire. This stern fourteenth century stronghold was built by Lord Scrope, Lord High Chancellor of England in the reign of Richard II.

Much of the great pile of masonry standing today is uninhabitable, but some of the extensive rooms are in use as a museum and a restaurant. The Scropes lived at Bolton Castle until 1630, the estate then passing to the Orde-Powletts family. But the most celebrated occupant was Mary Queen of Scots, who was held here as a prisoner for six months in 1568. With the help of the Duke of Norfolk she plotted to escape, not knowing that her notes to him were handed to Lord Burleigh before being passed on.

The title 'Windsor of the North' has been applied to Middleham Castle, sentinel of Wensleydale, as well as to Cawood Castle, near Selby, and as far as dimensions are concerned it certainly ranks as a serious claimant for such a distinction. Even in ruins, the massive proportions of the stronghold emphasise the importance it had in earlier days.

The great keep was erected in Norman times, but the heydays of the fortress began seven hundred years ago when the powerful

Bolton Castle, Wensleydale.

Middleham Castle.

Nevilles came on the scene and strengthened and extended it, making it the setting for great pageantry.

Charles Kingsley, author of *Westward Ho!*, *The Water Babies*, and other books was installed as a honorary canon of Middleham Church in 1845, and expressed his gratitude for the kindnesses he experienced on his visit.

But one custom observed at this place of workship in earlier days no longer took place in Kingsley's time. Until 1753, Middleham was a kind of Gretna Green, the parson here being privileged to perform marriage ceremonies without banns or licence.

Sir Walter Scott introduced Jervaulx Abbey into *Ivanhoe*, Prior Aylmer in the novel hailing from this monastery. A Cistercian retreat, it became rich during its four hundred years, until its leader, Abbot Adam Sedburgh, was executed for taking part in the insurrection called the Pilgrimage of Grace. He was imprisoned in the Tower of London, and his name can be seen scratched on a wall there before he was taken to his death at Tyburn in 1537.

The Autumnal sheep fair at Masham was for many years the highlight of Uredale life. Big flocks from various parts of the North Western Pennines converged on the moor behind the town, and the main topic of farmers' conversation related to Swaledales, Wensleydales, and crossbreds from these known as Mashams.

A curiosity in this restful town is a singular circular pillar in the parish churchyard. More than 6 feet high it is decorated with New Testament figures and is thought to be part of a huge cross set up more than a thousand years ago. Inside the same church is a painting of an angel in the sky, said to be part of a Nativity scene by Sir Joshua Reynolds and reputed to have been acquired for Masham Church after a fire at Belvoir Castle, Leicestershire.

So to Ripon, with the unparalleled Fountains Abbey, and Studley Park close by. Among Britain's ruined monasteries there are none quite in the same class as this superb structure, still entrancing in its disused state.

The lovely retreat occupies a plateau beside the little River Skell, that stream entering the Ure at Ripon, and helping to give Fountains Abbey its exquisite surroundings. In the early years of the twelfth century, the site was given to a band of twelve monks whose discontent with their life as Benedictines at St. Mary's Abbey, York, encouraged them to seek some spot where they could adopt the more severe rule of the Cistercians.

While making the foundations of their new abbey, they lived frugally in the shelter of a group of trees still pointed out to many of the visitors who marvel at the ruins every year. No matter whether they approach from the west, passing the attractive Jacobean house called Fountains Hall, or come more directly from Ripon through the pleasure grounds on the Studley Royal estate, the prospect of Fountains Abbey is incomparable.

In 1968 this outstandingly beautiful example of monastic architecture was bought by the West Riding County Council for restoration and preservation. The deal included more than six hundred acres of the Studley Royal property. Cared for as an Ancient Monument, under the wing of the Department of the Environment, Fountains is now the most popular treasure in Northern England.

The architecture of Ripon Cathedral was not always as it is today. Until the seventeenth century the towers carried spires. Nor do visitors realise that it owes much to Scottish enterprisee, the founders being monks from Melrose. But they built their Ripon monastery on a different site, and the cathedral we see today was begun when St. Wilfrid became abbot and moved the Roxburghshire occupants elsewhere. The present great church was inspired by him, and every August he is impersonated by a citizen of Ripon who rides through the streets on a white horse led by a monk.

The procession commemorates the return of the Saint from exile, to which he had condemned himself after a disagreement with the Archbishop of Canterbury. The Dean of Ripon today welcomes Wilfrid's arrival at the Cathedral, and there are prayers of thanksgiving for the Saint's foresight and influence on the history of the town.

America has tangible connections with the church and its surroundings. Wisconsin, U.S.A., has a place of the same name, and that American town has adopted the same civic slogan as its Yorkshire namesake—'Except ye Lord keepeth ye city, the Wakeman waketh in vain'. The Wakeman had the official duty of safeguarding the property of Ripon inhabitants from dusk until dawn, and during his period of office he lived in a house commanding the market place.

That old dwelling survives and has been restored to its ancient appearance. The medieval ritual of blowing a horn from the corners of the 90 feet high market cross at 9 p.m. each day continues too, and the custom is not suspended in summer, as happens at Bainbridge.

The strongest link between America and Ripon concerns 'Old Glory', the national flag of the U.S.A. There is a serious belief that the stars on that ensign are really five pointed spur wheels, like the ones produced in big quantities at Ripon, many of which reached North America and were in George Washington's mind when he designed the first all-America flag.

Probably the queerest object in Ripon today is a bell in the chapel of the original Hospital of St. Mary Magdalene, Stammergate. An eighteenth century Dean of the Cathedral had a great liking for port wine, but his stipend was too small for him to indulge as often as he wished. So he traded the hospital chapel bell for a case of his favourite tipple. When the loss of the bell was discovered, the Dean stated that it was being recast and would soon be returned. But he stressed that tolling it would be dangerous, and would most likely bring the bell crashing down on to the head of the bellringer.

Sure enough the bell was re-hung after a short absence, and the matter would have rested if some boys had not climbed on to the chapel roof in search of birds' nests. The young explorers reached the turret and found that the bell now hanging there would never ring. It was only a wooden replica.

Beside the Ure, and midway between Ripon and Boroughbridge, is one of Wren's masterpieces, Newby Hall, a fine example of a Queen Anne house. The mansion as we see it today was begun in 1705 and extended later in the same century. Now a stately home regularly open to the public, its treasures include work by Chippendale, Adam, and Zucchi. Another possession is a Gobelin tapestry made two hundred years ago by highly skilled weavers and needleworkers in France.

Skelton Church on the estate is an extremely colourful temple paid for by the mother of Frederick Grantham Vyner as a memorial after he had been killed by Greek brigands in 1870. An even more ornate church in his memory is Studley Royal Church, which can be seen on the way to Fountains Abbey from Ripon. Near to Newby Hall is one of Yorkshire's famous equestrian statues, originally created to commemorate the repelling of Ottoman invaders from Poland by troops supporting John Sobieski, monarch of that country. The statue was commissioned by the Polish Ambassador in London, but was never set up in the capital.

Sir Robert Vyner bought it and had it erected in Gautby Park, the Lincolnshire seat of the family. It was transferred to the grounds of Newby Hall in 1883, when a later Vyner inherited the Uredale property. A close examination of the figure will reveal that it is not entirely sculptured in Carrara marble, some repairs having been effected with painted wood!

Before uniting with the Swale, near Boroughbridge, to form the Ouse, the Ure flows within reach of those mysterious pillars known as the Devil's Arrows. They get their name from a tradition that they are bolts fired by Satan in an attempt to destroy Aldborough Church on the eastern side of Boroughbridge.

Standing as it does on the Great North Road, Boroughbridge was a busy station for coaches in the era of long distance horse-drawn traffic. Testimony to this fact are the old stables adjoining the large inns, though motor vehicles now replace the horses once stabled there.

Inhabitants of the town used to draw their water from a well reputed to be the deepest in the county. It is in St. James's Square, and descends 265 feet.

A cupola on pillars now protects the well, but it was in use as a communal source of water long before it was safeguarded by the addition of this structure in 1875, in memory of Andrew Lawson, of Aldborough Manor.

The historical importance of the well has since prompted a local preservation society to safeguard it for posterity, and to restore it to its original appearance. In bygone days there was much ornamental ironwork, and fortunately a number of photographs taken by a Boroughbridge plumber in 1900 show what the well looked like in the past.

If Satan failed to destroy Aldborough Church, the Romans certainly did not ignore the immediate surroundings, and the village has a place in history going back far beyond the early development of Boroughbridge. The church pulpit is supported by part of a Roman column, and the building has other Roman stones in its walls. Sites nearby have yielded mosaic floors made of Roman tiles.

The fourteenth century Battle of Boroughbridge may account for the slender clustered column on the village green at Aldborough, the pillar possibly having been erected to mark Edward II's victory over the Earl of Lancaster in a great clash of arms in the vicinity. For the collector of curiosities, Aldborough Church has a gravestone on which votes were counted at election times.

CHAPTER VII

Swaledale and Eskdale

Rising on opposite sides of Great Shunner Fell, and both turning their backs to Westmorland, the Ure and the Swale are companions as they make their way east across Yorkshire, uniting to form the economically more important River Ouse. As in many other instances, the Swale is not called by its familiar name throughout its length, and on the first stage of the journey is labelled Birkdale Beck.

Keld, a place of grey stone huddled in bare mountainous surroundings, is the highest of all populated spots in Swaledale, and at this point the valley is common referred to as Swaledale. There is nothing of much historic interest in Keld, although other placenames in the vicinity disclose that invaders from Norway once populated the region. They kept sheep on the fells in summer, and the suffix 'sett', as in Countersett and Marsett, is derived from the Norse 'Saetr' denoting a pasture used in summer. The geographical term 'seat', as in Rogan's Seat and Lovely Seat, given to the heights in various parts of Yorkshire, is of similar origin.

Always an isolated hamlet, Keld has become even more so in recent years. The Cathole Inn was converted into a house in 1954, and in 1955 the post office was transferred to an old shooting lodge, from which it was moved again after the building became a youth hostel.

Today the chief attraction lies in the glorious scenery surrounding it, and in the proximity to Kisdon Force a 30 foot waterfall. Living in a place encompassed by wild heights demands hardiness, and the robust physique of Keld folk was demonstrated by Edward Stillman, parson of the old chapel. Needing funds for repairs he set out to tramp to London begging money. He had a persuasive tongue as well as a strong body, and was as honest as any man, claiming only sixpence for his expenses when at last he walked back into his Swaledale parsonage, with enough cash to extend his chapel as well as to repair the building.

Two brothers who earned wide acclaim as naturalists, and pioneered bird photography, were born at Thwaite, between Keld and Muker. Richard and Cherry Kearton did not walk to London in search of helpers, but in their boyhood they did tramp to the school at Keld. Their daily journey introduced them to ornithology and kindled the spark which was later to fire a life-long passion for nature study.

The church at Muker dates from the reign of Elizabeth I, and is an odd little building. The narrow width, 22 feet, is disproportionate to its length, and the little tower only 8 feet square makes it still more a curiosity. It had a thatched roof until alterations were made in the eighteenth century. But the two bells are believed to have hung in Ellerton Priory near Reeth, farther down Swaledale. In that event they are older than the tower where they ring today. The church had a musicians gallery until 1890.

From Thwaite runs the road climbing over Abbotside Common to Hawes, a wild mountain highway linking Swaledale and Uredale. Named the Buttertubs Pass, it is close to the series of deep holes or natural tubs in the limestone, and takes its name from them.

Many of the rough tracks around Gunnerside show where eighteenth and nineteenth century lead miners walked to reach the shafts from which they extracted ore.

The capital of upper Swaledale is Reeth, though it is a much smaller place than the metropolis of the lower reaches of the valley, Richmond. Water taps on the green at Reeth have a strange story. Until 1868 the residents had only springs to provide them with water for drinking purposes. In that year, however, a benefactor in Richmond had supplies collected in a tank half a mile north of the green.

His name was George Robinson, and he was a member of a Reeth family occupying a big house there. The property subsequently became the Burgoyne Arms, and the last of the Robinsons to live there died sixty years ago. The tank remained in use when the local water supply was improved, and it became a supplementary source.

Parishioners from Reeth worship at Grinton beside the Swale, where the venerable church is a gem, the size and furnishings emphasing that it is more than a village church. The parish covers many miles of Swaledale, and at one time Bridlington Priory on the east coast had authority over this Dales edifice.

The Grinton locality was another lead mining area, and it is gratifying to know that a mine from those days is being preserved for posterity. It is within the Yorkshire Dales National Park, and this Grinton souvenir has been chosen for restoration as a tourist attraction because it has not been vandalised as much as other industrial ruins in the Park. It has some literary interest, too, appearing in Thomas Armstrong's book *Adam Brunskill.*

The ruins of two medieval nunneries share Swaledale views from different banks of the river on the way to Richmond. The tower and tumbled walls of Ellerton Priory occupy a site on the south bank, and Marrick Priory balances it on the north side. Both were founded about 1154, the latter by Lord Aske and the other by the Egglescliffe family.

Ellerton was a Cistercian nunnery and served that monastic order until the Dissolution, although it never acquired great riches, having a gross annual value of less than £16 when the nuns were set adrift. The church of Marrick Priory, built for Benedictine nuns, remained in use by the villagers of Marrick until a more convenient place of worship was acquired in 1893, but occasional services took place in the nave down to recent years.

Latterly, the interior, suitably adapted, became a centre for the Outward Bound organisation. Antiquarians should note that the present tower of the priory church is a reconstructed feature. The old structure was taken down in 1811 and then re-erected.

In attracting tourists, Richmond has several strings to its bow, a castle with a legend of buried treasure, the stately remnants of a Franciscan friary, a parish church uniquely incorporating shops, one of the most ungainly market crosses in the whole country, connections with a popular song, and a restored Georgian theatre where Edmund Kean and Harriet Mellon trod the boards at different times.

Alan the Red, a warrior related to the Duke of Brittany and a supporter of William of Normandy in the invasion and subjection of England nine hundred years ago, was granted 240 manors in North Yorkshire as his share of the booty. He was also entrusted with destroying any remaining insurgents fighting to regain the defeated King Harold's realm, and was also required to restore the economic life of the ravaged region.

In 1071 Alan began to build a stronghold, unique in conception at that period, which would be his private residence and administrative centre, as well as a military post for the defence of his properties and headquarters from which to harass rebels.

Unlike earlier Norman fortresses, this castle commanding Swaledale, was not built around a central keep or massive tower with encircling walls for its protection. Instead, Alan evolved a triangular plan with a keep near the apex. Richmond Castle in fact did not need to be completely surrounded by a curtain wall. The site was regarded as impregnable from the south because the gorge of the Swale on that side was a natural and perfect bastion.

This North Yorkshire fort also pioneers the use of stone instead of the earthen mounds and timber stockades common in the eleventh century. Few English castles built at that time can show masonry to a like degree as Richmond Castle.

The building known as Scolland's Hall, which Alan the Red erected in the south-east corner of the great court, has only one surviving parallel in Britain today, at Chepstow in Monmouthshire.

The legendary buried treasure centres round a story that when a secret tunnel was found, it was assumed to lead to a hidden cache of gold. The passage was too narrow for exploration by an adult, so a drummer boy was sent in and told to mark his progress by beating on his drum. The beats gradually faded to just a muffled rat-tat-tat, and the lad was never seen again, though it is said that the sounds of distant drumming are still to be heard beneath the castle. It is remarkable how natural phenomena, such as dripping water, can create sounds which help to perpetuate old legends!

Another story about this stronghold cannot be explained in that way. It describes how a simple potter discovered an entrance which led him to a large underground chamber where King Arthur and his knights lay sleeping until they are summoned by a magic horn to awaken in the defence of England at a time of natural peril. Arthur's sword, Excalibur, lay nearby, and the potter rashly tried to steal it. No sooner did he touch it than the knights stirred, and their armour clanged as they awoke and cried out 'Is it time?'.

As the terrified disturber of Arthurian peace fled, a mocking voice fell on his ears, saying:

> Potter, Peter Thompson,
> If thou hadst either drawn

The sword or blown the horn,
Thou wouldst have been the luckiest man
That ever yet was born.

One account states that he was made aware of the cave in a vision. Despite frantic attempts to find the entrance again, he never succeeded.

There is strong support for the belief that the composer of 'The Lass of Richmond Hill' had this Yorkshire town in mind and not its Surrey namesake. The verses are generally conceded to have been written by Leonard McNally in praise of Miss Anson of Hill House, Richmond, Yorkshire, before she became Mrs. McNally.

The Surrey town of Richmond became involved when the Yorkshire couple went to that neighbourhood, Leonard McNally being a Londoner. James Hook, who composed the music, had a number of his works performed in Richmond, Surrey, which has added to the confusion.

In quaintly named Friars Wynd is a unique Georgian theatre, built by Samuel Butler in 1788. It has not been in continuous service as a place of entertainment, having served as a warehouse for a number of years, but its original interior has been restored. Among other famous actors and actresses who performed here are John Kemble and Sarah Siddons.

Friars Wynd refers to a friary built in 1258 by followers of St. Francis of Assisi. The beautiful tower is still an architectural gem, though the friary has been unused and in ruins for four hundred years.

It was not a monastic retreat, but a centre from which the Grey Friars went out to perform widespread duties. They served as missionaries, performed miracle plays, and gave homely sermons. Several were slain when they refused to vacate the friary after opposing Henry VIII's edict confiscating their property, while others were imprisoned.

There is nowhere in the country to compare with Holy Trinity Church, so far as its secular usages are concerned. Since 1740 it has incorporated a number of shops, being built to replace the south aisle. Assize courts and consistory courts were held in the north aisle, and local inhabitants made their home in the church at times of plague, believing that there they could escape the pestilence.

St. Mary's churchyard, Frenchgate, has a memento of the same tragic days, a stone marking the mass grave where some of the victims were buried. This church supplanted Holy Trinity Church as the Parish Church of Richmond. Both buildings date back eight hundred years, but St. Mary's was rebuilt in 1958–9, with the exception of the twelfth century arcades and medieval north doorway. The west tower dates from the middle of the fifteenth century.

This is the garrison church of the Green Howards regiment, their banners being displayed in the south side memorial chapel.

Other treasures in St. Mary's include a series of wooden stalls salvaged from Easby Abbey. Carved in the sixteenth century, one depicts piglets dancing to music played on bagpipes by a pig. Further misereres warn against sins such as scandal-mongering, quarrelling in holy places, and creating disorders in the choir.

The unprepossessing column in the market place marks the site of the original cross.

Easby Abbey is just over a mile from Richmond, a pleasant walk from the town along the riverside. The White Canons who came here in 1152 did not build around the little church already standing there, but gave their abbey its own church, leaving the old one to continue unmolested. Easby, though only a cluster of houses, boasts both an engaging monastery and an even older church.

A great number of the Scrope family lie in the church, their armorial bearings adorning the porch, together with those of the Askes and the Conyers, all powerful families in past times. The interior surfaces of the church are decorated with paintings dating from the thirteenth century, excelled only by the medieval mural art in Pickering parish church.

The ancient cross of Easby Church was found in fragments, some in the walls of the church itself, and others on private property. When the pieces were put together again, the Victoria and Albert Museum expressed a wish to have the cross, and a plaster cast of it was provided. This replica is seen in Easby Church today.

The beginnings of the Abbey are attributed to Roald, Constable of Richmond Castle, who had the foundations laid in 1152. The Scropes came into possession some two hundred years later, continuing the responsibility and bequeathing money for the maintenance.

In our time the Government has done much to clean the site, the ground plan being disclosed, and the stream which passes by on its way to join the Swale still races by as merrily as it did in the heydays of the monastery, although some years ago it was harnessed to supply electricity.

One of the Scropes plotted to kill Henry V on his way to France, but the conspirators met disaster and execution when their treachery was revealed, as related in Shakespeare's play.

The Esk is the only Yorkshire river of real importance which flows almost directly eastwards to empty into the North Sea. Rising in the Cleveland Hills, it gives Eskdale its name, and follows a winding course from the vicinity of Castleton, through delightful country before reaching Whitby after a twenty-one mile journey.

Despite the remote situation, Castleton has long been a market town, at a convenient point for roads running along the much smaller valleys of Commondale, Westerdale, Sleddale, and Baysdale.

The connections between the town and the outlaws of Sherwood Forest in Nottingham, are uncertain, but a local inn is named after Robin Hood.

Castleton Church is a modern one built as a memorial to men who fell in the Great War, much of the oak furnishings having been carved with an adze, a tool widely used in olden days. The castle which gave the town its name was built by the Bruces in the Norman period, though only the site can now be traced. The surviving parts are incorporated in a farmstead, but two towers overlook the courtyard, and another feature is a dungeon with a vaulted roof and dark entrance.

Danby parish church, with its squat tower over the south porch, owes much to Canon Atkinson, who went there in 1847. His book *Forty Years in a Moorland Parish* was a best-seller. He died in 1900, lying in the graveyard of the church he served, and which he helped greatly to restore.

Half a mile north of Danby Castle the Esk is spanned by Duck Bridge, which is only $6\frac{1}{2}$ feet wide and was designed for pack pony transport, and not for wheeled traffic. It was originally known as Danby Castle Bridge, and retained that title for some four hundred years before being renamed in honour of George Duck who paid generously towards its reconstruction in 1717.

Beggar's Bridge, near the hamlet of Glaisdale, was built by Thomas Ferris of Hull, who made his fortune by helping to capture a galleon laden with rich cargo in the Spanish Main. He built the bridge as a reminder to his earlier days when he was poor, and secretly meeting the local squire's daughter, only to be sent away by her father, who did not consider him good enough. When he returned a rich man, he was allowed to marry her.

The bridges at Egton and Sleights were washed away by floods in 1930, both having existed since the sixteenth century, though from time to time being washed away.

Grosmont, named after the Normandy abbey from which monks came to Eskdale, has a font in the village church thought to date from this time. The ironworkings in and around the village causing unsightly slag heaps have marred the beauty of the place, but the heaps are dwindling now that their contents have been used in road building.

Downstream, the valley becomes a captivating glen, and the surrounding heights are reached by climbing Blue Bank, at one time difficult for motorists. From the top there is a panoramic view of Whitby and neighbourhood.

Over eight hundred years ago a hermit lived in a cell on the bank of the Esk just outside Sleights, where he gave refuge to a wild boar which was being hunted by three local barons. The angry hunters slew the hermit and the boar, but before he died the recluse asked the Abbot of Whitby to spare his assassins' lives provided they did

Whitby Abbey.

Whitby Harbour, looking across to St. Hilda's Abbey and St. Mary's Church.

penance each Ascension Day. They were required to cut stakes and repair the wooden quay at Whitby, building a symbolic hedge capable of withstanding three tides. This rite believed to have been first enacted in 1160, continues annually, and is known as The Planting of the Penny Hedge. The name refers not to coinage, the name Penny being a corruption of penance.

Whitby is firstly a port, but is also a popular holiday resort, and has an entertaining history. It has been a seaport since Elizabethan days, and later many whalers were built there. The Whitby whaling fleet at one period totalled fifty ships, their average catch being over fifty whales each season. Large numbers of seals were landed, and even bears from the Far North.

Whitby has many reminders of Captain Cook, who chose a boat built there, the *Resolution*, for his voyage of discovery to the South Seas in 1772. There is a small house in Grape Lane where he lived as an apprentice and studied seamanship in the attic. Pannet Park Museum contains an enchanting collection of objects associated with him, and the weathervane on Westcliffe is a model of the *Resolution*. Nearby is a bronze statue, showing him with compass in hand, and a chart tucked under one arm.

St. Hilda's Abbey was founded in 657, the most unusual feature being that it accommodated both men and women. It is built on a wold cliff and was destroyed by the Danes in 867–70.

St. Mary's parish church, near the Abbey has galleries like the bridge of a ship. The pews are all shapes and sizes, and the woodwork is painted white.

Nearby stand an old, plain market cross and a wonderfully ornamented modern column showing scenes from the life of the swineherd, Caedmon, the Father of English Sacred Song.

CHAPTER VIII

York and Beyond

Captivating, historically exciting, impressive, and incomparable, these are all terms merited by York, and they are applicable to a degree unmatched elsewhere in the United Kingdom.

Cathedrals up and down the country bear witness to the genius of architects and the skill of craftsmen in bygone centuries. Various other cities and towns have Roman remains, monastic structures, medieval almshouses, sections of old walls, ancient portals, venerable parish churches, and castles founded hundreds of years ago.

Yet none of these centres of population has such a rich and varied collection as York. The Minster is the biggest church in England, dwarfing St. Paul's in London, and the northern city embraces the largest number of churches in any one place in England, eighteen in all. York is indeed incomparable, the souvenirs from past centuries being so numerous that it is impossible to stand at any point inside the boundaries without having some engaging historical object in sight.

The Minster itself is a storeplace for a wide range of mementoes, apart from its architectural glories and the priceless window glass. It began as a wooden temple more than thirteen hundred years ago, Edwin, the first Christian King of Northumbria, being baptised in the oratory. The exact date is uncertain, but the event is believed to have occurred in AD 627.

Six years after his baptism, Edwin was slain by the heathen King Penda of Mercia, and the stone church which Edwin had begun at York to replace the wooden one, encountered dark days, until Penda himself suffered defeat and death in AD 655. From that year the history of the Minster has been one of continuity.

Another Saxon church followed, and a fourth was built by Archbishop Thomas of Bayeux, the first part being completed soon after the Norman Conquest. Unfortunately this edifice was seriously damaged by fire in 1137, the blaze also destroying much of the surrounding property.

The job of rebuilding the Minster was accepted by Archbishop Roger, and after lying in ruins for many years the first part of the new church was completed in 1241. This was the basis of the splendid pile we see today, except for the towers, which were not erected until well into the fifteenth century, and the present-day south-west one replaces a forerunner razed by fire in 1840.

This was the second occasion in the nineteenth century when a disaster of that kind struck the Minster, the choir being completely gutted when a man set it ablaze in February 1829. Nearly all the medieval carved furniture, including the archbishop's throne, was destroyed. Two of the stalls which survived, however, can be inspected in the Zouche Chapel, a part of the building which demonstrates the diversity of the souvenirs to be found in the Minster, and illustrates that the attractions are not confined to architecture, magnificently conceived though it obviously was.

In a corner of the Chapel is an ancient well, complete with windlass and bucket, and close by is a plaque bearing a biblical carving with an unusual history. It is one of a pair executed by an unknown Flemish woodcarver about the year 1660. Their whereabouts from that date until Victorian days are obscure, but they were built into a mantelpiece of a house owned by the father of the Suffragan Bishop of Whitby, and were left to York Minster in 1953.

The companion carving shows the Conversion of Saint Paul, and is now in the north aisle of the choir. It is of exceptional interest because the sculptor has carved a camel in the procession to Damascus, an animal which he had obviously never seen.

The Zouche Chapel containing the other plaque is part of a chapel provided in the will of Archbishop La Zouche in 1351. The accommodation is now used for private prayer and meditation.

The story that the lovely fire-lancet window known as the 'Five Sisters' was the conception of five young ladies of the neighbourhood, who first designed it as a work of tapestry and then had it made in coloured glass, is romantic but unsubstantiated. Nevertheless, the windows do contain the finest collection of thirteenth century grisaille glass in existence, and included is a unique fragment of Norman glass depicting Daniel in the lion's den.

The whole ensemble contains one hundred thousand pieces, and an aspect not apparent to the ordinary beholder is that they are set in seven hundred years old lead from Rievaulx Abbey. These historic windows, along with most of the other medieval ones, were removed and stored for safety during the Second World War, but they have been progressively replaced. At the same time the opportunity has been taken to ensure that the contents of panels wrongly rearranged in earlier restorations are as originally intended.

Even more superb than the 'Five Sisters' window is the great east window, a veritable wall of glass, and the largest stained window in the world. The 144 divisions show saints, angels, biblical characters, scenes from the Testaments, and kings and queens portrayed in 1,700 square feet of glass which dates from the fifteenth century. Yet, the designer, John Thornton of Coventry, was paid only £55 for working on this stupendous creation from 1405–8!

The Minster abounds in lesser but none the less engaging treasures, such as the Horn of Ulphus, Canute's son-in-law. Believing that his two sons would quarrel over their legacies when he died, Ulphus solemnly provided for his estates to pass to the Minster. Visiting the shrine, he knelt before the altar and drank wine from the Horn, dedicating all his properties and their revenues for the use of the See of York 'for ever'.

As a symbol of this arrangement, the $2\frac{1}{2}$ foot long drinking horn became a prized possession of the Minster, although it was stolen at the time of the Reformation and its whereabouts were uncertain for many years. Soon after the Civil War, however it came into the hands of Sir Thomas Fairfax the Parliamentary general who returned it to the See in 1674.

Today it is on view in the Undercroft. Apart from the link with Ulphus, Prince of Deira (later part of Northumbria), it is of overseas interest, possibly having been made in Persia and reaching England through Russia and Denmark, where drinking horns were used as title deeds to property. Ulphus's Horn is made of ivory, and is probably part of a mammoth's tusk. Mythical beasts are carved on the outside, together with an inscription, but the gold mountings were removed by a London goldsmith while it was in obscurity.

More city gateways are in use in York today than anywhere else in the country, despite the extent to which they constrict modern road traffic. The most suitable way to see them is to walk along the city walls, which encircle the old parts, except for a stretch near the River Foss, where the natural defences sufficed.

Both Monk Bar and Bootham Bar are near the Minster, and

access to the pedestrian route round the walls can be obtained at these points. Monk Bar consists of a Norman arch protected by an iron-toothed oak portcullis complete with the medieval machinery for raising and lowering this barrier. Like all the other York portals, except Walmgate Bar it has lost its outer barbican or tunnel-like structure which concentrated attackers into a narrow space, but the formidable nature of the various bars in medieval warfare is evident. Walmgate Bar is unique because it also bears a house added in Tudor times.

It guarded the approach from the East Coast, while Bootham Bar gave protection from the North. At Bootham Bar it was usual to hire guides and guards for journeys through the thick and menacing forests on the way to Thirsk and farther north. Stone figures on the battlements of this and other ancient York portals have been described either as representing saints whose help was sought in defending the city, or as hoax soldiers intended to hoodwink attackers and make them less likely to launch as assault.

Most grim of all the fortified entrances to the old city is Micklegate Bar, for on it were displayed the severed heads of vanquished warriors and alleged traitors. The most famous figure to suffer this

Walmgate Bar, York.

fate was the ill-starred Duke of York, slain at the Battle of Wake-field in 1460. Lord Salisbury's head was also stuck on a pole over the gateway, but both were removed when the Lancastrians were beaten at York by the Yorkists in 1461, and the Duke's son became Edward IV.

There have been gruesome events at York Castle too. In 1090, when the Conqueror sought to subdue the local population, about five hundred Jews took refuge in a wooden fortress on the site of the present stone-built Clifford's Tower. They perished when flames destroyed the building though it is not now certain that the fires were deliberately started.

The stone stronghold was built seven hundred years ago, and nearby in the one-time prison, is an attraction which lures as many visitors as the Minster. Known as the Castle Museum, it is not a general collection of exhibits, but one of the most popular Folk Museums in Britain.

Here is a re-created street with shops and workplaces, complete to small details. It is a place of nostalgia for the elderly as well as one of education for the young.

One of the most remarkable events in the city's long history concerns St. Mary's Abbey, substantial remains of which can be explored near Lendal Bridge. This retreat, the first monastic house established in Yorkshire after the Norman Conquest, was a Benedictine abbey.

The rules of St. Benedict were strictly imposed and stern penalties were prescribed for violations. When a certain Brother Jocundus erred seriously he was sentenced to be immured in an outer wall, and left to die. He was walled in as prescribed, and after a time his presence there as a corpse was regarded as certain.

There was consternation when, weeks later, Jocundus miracu-lously emerged from his vertical tomb as hale and as hearty as ever he had been! But the incident wasn't the miraculous happening it was at first assumed to be. The outer wall of St. Mary's Abbey was shared with an adjoining monastery, and the guilty monk had emerged secretly into that other retreat soon after being walled up. He had joined in the activities of these other brethren until he had offended *their* code of conduct, and been sentenced again to be immured! This time he had reversed his previous experience, coming back into the monastery from which he had originally been banished.

Once called 'Altera Roma', or a second Rome, York was developed as the chief North of England city during the Roman Occupation largely as a military centre, while London served for trading. The Romans had two of their 'crack' legions here, where Roman emperors were proclaimed, and where troops were stationed to control the unsubdued tribes north of the Humber.

Today the city is rich in reminders of those days, many Roman remains having been dug up, and the list is still being increased. Items of this sort are in profusion in the Museum near Lendal Bridge, and the nearby multiangular tower was the western corner of the Roman fort defending the military station. It is believed to have been admired by the Emperor Constantine, who died at York in AD 306. Among other Emperors who came to the city were Hadrian, responsible for the great Wall named after him, and Serverus, who came as an ailing figure to die at York, and to give his name to a hill near the present suburb of Acomb, on which his body was burned.

In the Middle Ages the city became a big trading centre. Witness to this are the trade guilds set up there to control individual trades and professions; the weavers, the tailors and in particular the merchant adventurers. This last named fraternity consisted largely of traders in woollen goods and mercer's items, and although the official title of their organisation was The Company of Merchant Adventurers of the City of York, it has also been known as the Mercers' Guild.

No fewer than three medieval guildhalls exist in York today— those of the Merchant Adventurers', the Merchant Tailors' or Taylors', and the St. Anthony's Guild, the last-named having been founded as a religious fraternity in 1446 and dissolved in 1627. St. Anthony's Hall was also used by small guilds which had no meeting place of their own.

The Guildhall where civic matters were debated as long ago as 1726, and which stands near the Lord Mayor's official residence, the Mansion House, also survived until it was badly damaged by an enemy bomb in 1942. It was not irreparably harmed, however, and has been carefully restored.

The city's churches merit a study, whether from the historical angle, the architectural viewpoint, or just for the curiosities they harbour. St. Olave's, immediately to the north of St. Mary's Abbey, contains a feature found in no other church. A pew near the east end of the nave is fitted with a special rest for a parishioner's peg leg!

St. Michael-le-Belfry's Church, in the shadow of the Minster, has the name of Guy Fawkes in its parish registers, this being the place of his baptism. Holy Trinity Church, Micklegate, may be described as a cannibalised building, its tower having been moved there from the now vanished St. Nicholas's Church. Holy Trinity Church, Goodramgate, is in a little sequestered spot, but is visited chiefly for its assortment of box pews, the leaning walls and arches, and the different floor levels. All in all, it lives up to its reputation as a nightmarish church or a scene from some crazy cartoon.

Best-known of York's streets from the Middle Ages are the oddly named Whip-Ma-Whop-Ma Gate, believed to have derived its title from an occasion when a dog was chased from the nearby Church of St. Crux, or possibly from the flaying of convicted criminals hereabouts, and the extraordinarily narrow Shambles with timber framed houses nodding to each other from either side. The origins of this thoroughfare are more readily understood if its earlier name of Fleshammels is borne in mind as this refers to the time when butchers' stalls occupied the vicinity.

Few people, however, see another ancient street or are even aware of its existence, because it runs underground from the Ouse near the Guildhall towards St. Helen's Square and Stonegate. The subterranean route, open to the sky before the Guildhall was built over it, was used for the transport of materials from river barges to the Minster when that shrine was being erected and extended.

To stroll round the city walls with an alert eye is to become acquainted with life as it existed there at various periods. The inhabitants in medieval days were highly superstitious, and an illustration of this is to be found in Stonegate. A frightful image of Satan sits high up above a shop which was once a dwelling house. He is shown securely chained, in accordance with the belief that such a manacled figure would deter the real Prince of Darkness from attempting to enter the house.

Reminders of more gracious days are the torch snuffers outside some other York houses, notably in the neighbourhood of Duncombe Place and the Georgian-style Assembly Rooms, still resplendent from the era when York rivalled Bath as a resort for the aristocracy. Because no civic street lighting was available at that period, torch carriers were hired to accompany revellers along the dark streets, and they used the big snuffers outside some of the entrances to extinguish their torches.

The main route northwards from York towards Easingwold and Thirsk skirts Skelton, a village just outside the city with Minster associations other than proximity to that impressive pile. Tradition says that masons engaged on the Minster had some stones left when they built the transepts there, so they took the materials to Skelton and erected the village church, to demonstrate their interest in humble shrines as well as in splendid cathedrals.

The back thoroughfare of Easingwold is aptly named Long Street, and though road traffic today speeds past the town almost unheedingly, the quiet quarters are worth observing. It is a market town with gracious greens and a cobbled market place adjoining a big roofed area around the market cross.

Coxwold, east of the Easingwold–Thirsk road, owes its fame to the eighteenth-century humorist, Laurence Sterne, parson of the village. Shandy Hall, now a showplace, was his home for the last eight years of his life, and here he wrote *The Sentimental Journey,* and finished *Tristram Shandy,* two of the immortal works in English literature.

One of England's hillside wonders, the Kilburn White Horse, is a landmark on the slope of the Hambleton Hills, and is visible from many vantage points. Cut in the turf in 1857 by a local schoolmaster and his pupils, and then used, it is said, for measuration lessons, the animal is 314 feet long and 228 feet high, and twenty persons can sit together on the eye. The creature is 'groomed' at intervals so that it remains conspicuous, though various methods such as the spreading of glass on the surface have not succeeded in eleminating entirely the need for periodic attention.

Fame has come to Kilburn in quite a different way this century. In a workshop here the late Robert Thompson established the craft of ecclesiastical woodcarving, and examples of fine workmanship from this rural place are now to be seen in countless churches. The items are easily identifiable by the mouse symbol carved on them.

There is unlikely to be any truth in the belief that Thirsk parish church was built partly with materials from Thirsk Castle, that stronghold having been an earth and timber affair destroyed in the twelfth century, whereas the church is entirely of fifteenth-century origin so far as the general architecture is concerned.

It is, indeed, rare for that reason, most other churches displaying mixtures of architectural style or influence.

As a much used halt in coaching days the town is well-provided with inns and posting stations, and is a popular marketing centre today, though the ancient market cross is now in the grounds of the home of the lord of the manor.

North-east from York, and leading to Filey and Scarborough, is the A64, a strange highway in one sense. On the eighteen miles between York and Malton, not a single village of any unusual importance is negotiated. Today the route with well defined traffic lanes speeds motorists from York to the Malton bottleneck. However, a feature to see is the fluted column visible above the trees on the skyline from the foot of Whitwell Bank, twelve miles from York.

The pillar crowns Bulmer Hill and was erected at the expense of workers and tenants on the Castle Howard estates. Costing them £2,000, it was put up in memory of the seventh Earl of Carlisle, Lord Morpeth, who served as Viceroy of Ireland for eight years. The memorial used to have a cupola which reflected the rays of the sun, thus creating a lighted torch effect across the Vale of York.

It also marks the southern end of the mile long avenue, punctuated by gateways, on the way to the stately Castle Howard erected by the third Earl of Carlisle. The work began in 1699, following the ideas of Sir John Vanburgh, and was ready for use in 1726.

Horace Walpole was enchanted by the splendour and size, stating 'Nobody had informed me that at one view I should see a palace, a town, a fortified city, temples on high places, woods worthy of being each a metropolis of the Druids, the noblest lawn in the world fenced by half the horizon, and a mausoleum that would tempt one to be buried alive. In short, I have seen gigantic places before, but never a sublime one.'

The ordinary populace have been thrilled in much the same way at Castle Howard for some two hundred and fifty years, this spectacular pile having been open to the public long before the twentieth century custom of giving access to our stately homes gained widespread support.

A winding but more pleasant alternative route connects York and Malton, taking the motorist along the delightful Derwent

Valley via Gate Helmsley, Buttercrambe, Scrayingham, Kirkham, Low Hutton, and Welham. Not to be confused with the River Derwent near the East Coast, this attractive waterway bearing the same name flows parallel to the modern, village-free highway already described, and is infinitely preferable.

The ruins of the Augustinian abbey of Kirkham nestle serenely six miles from Malton. Officially it was a priory, though often marked on maps as an abbey, the tenants not being confined to a cloistered life, but leaving their centre to carry out parochial duties within the surrounding area.

Legend declares that the Derwent Valley priory was founded in 1122 in memory of Walter d'Espec's son. The youth was killed when thrown from his horse, his head striking a boulder—the rock, so it is said, being the one still in position in front of the gateway.

The entrance is now the most extensive part of the ruins, and bears coats-of-arms representing various illustrious families formerly connected with the priory. But Kirkham has lost a custom which was almost unique in the North Riding, an annual Bird Fair. The ritual did not cease until towards the end of the nineteenth century, and up to that time many species of bird were brought to Kirkham each Trinity Sunday and were sold for cash or exchanged for goods.

There are two Maltons, the old and the new, and it is the new town which frustrates motorists, but the old one which Charles Dickens knew. He was a guest of his friend Charles Smithson, at Easthope Hall, three miles away, while touring North Yorkshire in search of information for *Nicholas Nickleby*.

The term 'old' is apt for the part of the township on the way to Pickering. It has a striking priory church founded for Gilbertine canons more than eight hundred years ago. Today it is the only surviving church of the English Order of St. Gilbert still in use for regular divine worship, though five similar priories established in Yorkshire alone.

The central tower of Malton Priory was razed in 1636, and the choir was demolished in 1734. It had two western towers, but there is now only one. The crypt is underneath the nearby Cross Keys Inn. Of special interest inside the building are a wealth of misereres or choir seat carvings. They include various animals and birds, the strangest being a dromedary.

If this collection is insufficient to support the claim that this area of Malton is really old, evidence of the existence of a Roman fort has been unearthed in a nearby field, and is marked by a monument.

Reference to Malton's traffic headaches prompts the belief that our Yorkshire ancestors were long ago aware of the harassment created by long distance transport in other parts of the country, when the internal combustion engine was not even dreamed about.

The suggestion arises from the realisation that several of the villages between Malton and Scarborough do not use the main road as their High Street as we might expect. Instead, they were built along a side road at right angles to the important busy highway.

Support for the notion that this was a definite policy is obtainable from a large scale map, which discloses that the side tracks lead to no other place, being cul-de-sacs with little except farmland beyond the village.

Examples in this class along the Malton–Scarborough road, are Rillington, West Heslerton (though its main street does develop into a secondary lane to Yedingham on the other side of the Malton–Scarborough railway line), East Heslerton, and Sherburn. In consequence the inhabitants of these places are spared much of the rumble and hurly-burly of vehicles going to and from the north-east coast, yet are almost on the main route whenever they wish to use it.

On the other hand, the parishioners of Rillington appear to have been less easily upset by noise than were many other villagers. They did not worship in some quiet spot, but in a church on a mound beside the bustling main road. Their shrine must be even noisier today, cars roaring past continuously while services are being held.

The congregations have an opportunity to study some seven hundred years old wall paintings on the north aisle, and on the south wall outside the building is an inscription to a Scampston man, Matthew Pape, which implies that honesty was rare in the eighteenth century.

Sherburn Church, however, lies well away from the motorists' route, but is nevertheless part of the village and is worth inspecting for its carved woodwork. There is old and new, and the craft of the ancient woodcarver can be compared with the skill of his modern counterpart.

Staxton is the spot where the road divides for Filey and Scarborough respectively. A relic displayed in a garden plot adjoining the platform at Seamer station on the way to Scarborough, is singular among objects on show in railway surroundings.

In the Ice Age, when glaciers scoured the landscape, a large boulder was deposited at Seamer, and is now preserved in the way just described.

Look in the church for the memorial to Richard Wilson. It shows in relief the seamen's home which he presented to Scarborough.

The resort calls itself a queenly place, and few visitors would quarrel with that. Yet the discovery of medicinal springs, which led to development as a watering place, and the erection of a special building for those 'taking the waters', occurred as long ago as 1620. The construction of the first 'Spaw House' was completed eighty years later and visitors both imbibed the health-giving drinks and indulged in the (then) new activity of sea-bathing.

The Spa House of those days was a wooden affair reached by climbing a ladder from the beach, but the waves often damaged the buildings and the structures had to undergo frequent repairs. The present Spa with its ballroom, theatre, restaurant and other facilities gradually evolved after a fire destroyed their immediate forerunners in 1876, and later conflagrations completed the destruction.

Yet Scarborough's rise as 'Queen of Watering places' was threatened quite differently in 1735. In that year a landslide diverted the springs, and the worried townsfolk sought the new channels, fearing that the resort would soon be shunned if no curative waters were available. Fortunately, the springs eventually found again, and the inhabitants breathed once more. Was their anxiety necessary? The question may be asked because the Spa does not now have medicinal waters available, and the town has not suffered a decline as a result of their absence.

So far from restricting its appeal as a health resort, Scarborough retains profitable reminders of other days and different pursuits. The neighbouring area was subjugated by the Romans, and bombarded from the sea and air during the Great War.

The long-held idea that the Romans established themselves in the region lacked proof until 1923. In that year the substantial remains of a Roman signal station were discovered on a mound near the castle. The massive foundations revealed that they must have supported a tower of at least eighty feet high.

The privateer, John Paul Jones, who became the first great hero of the American navy, met defeat off Flamborough Head in 1779. The affray between his ships and those of the Royal Navy ended when the American flagship under Jones's command was sunk.

In the Great War the resort came under bombardment from warships, and in earlier times kings and rebels have fought in the streets or attacked the castle. The stronghold, on a cliff three hundred feet above the sea, was regarded as impregnable, and it is true that the fortress was never captured by storm. It fell only as a result of siege.

The religious insurrections at the beginning of Queen Mary's reign caused Scarborough Castle to be taken by trickery on the part of attackers led by Thomas Stafford. On market days local traders were allowed to approach the gateway in order to offer their wares to the garrison. So Stafford dressed some of his followers as dealers, but their baskets contained weapons instead of produce.

As soon as the 'tradesmen' entered the castle they overpowered the sentries and captured it. Nevertheless the victory was short-lived, the stronghold being retaken three days later and Stafford taken to London for execution.

The best-kept part of the structure today is the entrance where the traders appeared, the rounded side-towers being impressive. From the inside grounds a fine view of the coastline and Scarborough presents itself. The panorama includes St. Mary's Church, where Anne Brontë sleeps in the separate graveyard east of the building.

She died in 1849, having gone to the east coast in the hope of recovering from illness. Her burial place and grave slab are now well tended by admirers of the Brontë sisters.

In the days before Scarborough began to develop as a 'Brighton of the North', it was a haunt of smugglers. One of their meeting places and the spot where they congregated to discuss their plans to get contraband ashore, and arrange for its dispersal to inland

Anne Brontë's grave at Scarborough.

centres, is the old Three Mariners' Inn, with secret cupboards and other aids for freebooting.

It stands in a narrow alley near the harbour, and in the same locality is a more readily noticed fourteenth century building known as Richard III's house because he is thought to have lodged there. A stone effigy behind a grille is reputed to represent the crookbacked king.

The premises today are just a wing of a much larger dwelling on the same site, but even this section is attractive. The bed-chamber thought to have been occupied by Richard has a remarkable ceiling made by Italian craftsmen nearly five hundred years ago. A curious ornamentation is a trio of rabbits, each animal being so arranged that it has two ears although there are really only three among them.

The harbour nowadays provides berths and anchorages for many pleasure craft amid the cobles, drifters, and other vessels. None-the-less, it is easy to take one's mind back down the years and imagine the time here before the town became a resort. In those days two hundred herring boats sailed into the port as the shoals were followed along the North Sea. The vessels came from other eastern and north-eastern places, and many were the dialect tongues heard on Scarborough's foreshore.

The curtailment of the herring fisheries was one of the most important factors influencing the growth of the town as a holiday centre. When one door was closed until it was no more than ajar, another one opened with the expansion of railways, and it has been thrust well back as the growth of motoring has encouraged still more people to converge upon this historic and attractive Yorkshire watering-place.

CHAPTER IX

Along the Yorkshire Coast

It is hard to imagine that the boomerang-shaped range of chalk hills known as the Yorkshire Wolds, today an important granary, were a rabbit-ridden wilderness not much more than a century ago. Where bracken and warrens existed at that time, golden corn now presents an alluring picture each autumn, and thriving trees form windbreaks for prosperous looking farmsteads.

The instigators of the transformation were the Sykes family of Sledmere, who developed the region into valuable agricultural land.

The pioneer was Sir Christopher Sykes, who planted hedges and made roads in the hitherto open country, encouraging cottagers to graze their cattle on the roadside verges as part of his wide-embracing scheme to turn rough land into cornfields.

The good work was continued by his son, Sir Tatton Sykes, whose horses were the best hunters of the day, and whose breeds of sheep were nationally known. He brought a semi-scientific skill to farming the Wolds, being the first to realise the value of bone meal as manure, and the inventor of the original bone-crushing machine.

His experiments in this direction arose from his noticing that the grass grew thickest and strongest around kennels where dogs buried their bones. A perfect country squire, he was not averse to lending a hand with ploughing, reaping, and other necessary farmland activities.

He was proud of his family seat, Sledmere House, and extended it. The present mansion, now a stately home open to the public, is not the one where he lived, however. It is a replica erected after a disastrous fire in 1911.

Another glory of the village is the splendid cross, modelled after an Eleanor cross, in memory of the Green Howards. It was built by Sir Tatton Sykes in 1900, and adopted as a Great War monument, with brass portraits of local men who did not return from the holocaust. A stumpy memorial commemorates the twelve hundred-strong Wolds Waggoners, raised by Sir Mark Sykes, and has a series of panels depicting wartime events. The scenes remarkably illustrate such occasions as the embarkation of troops, and the retreat from Mons.

It is convenient to follow the Wolds from Bridlington to their southern extremity near the Humber, then visiting Hull and Beverley, with offshoots to smaller but engaging places along the coastline, or a few miles inland.

A new store at Bridlington, built for £500,000, pays the landlords an annual rent of only seventeen 'old' shillings. That is the amount fixed for the site by the historic Lords of Feoffees, governors of the town, a body founded in the seventeenth century to control market fees, and perform other local administration functions. The ancient courtroom, where the twenty-five freeholders still meet to debate, is in the Bayle Gate, which in olden days guarded entry to Bridlington, or Burlington, Priory until that rich Augustinian centre was destroyed after Prior William Wode had been a supporter of the Pilgrimage of Grace, for which offence he was executed at Tyburn in 1537.

From these circumstances, it will be clear that the Bridlington of today, attracting many holidaymakers each summer, has a double character. The original town is well inland and is almost severed from the coastal resort. The church used in the heydays of the Priory serves as the parish church of the older place, and the twin towers are a landmark at sea, as well as from the surrounding villages.

Among the earliest occupants of the Priory was the alchemist George Ripley, who spent his life in a futile quest for the 'philosopher's stone' which, it was widely thought, would turn base metals into gold. His burial place is in the church.

Altogether there were thirty-one priors at Bridlington between the founding of the community in 1113, and the suppression in 1539. A graveslab refers to William Bower, who died in 1671, and who had a knitting school in the town. His charity helped to provide the new buildings of Bridlington School.

As a seaside town, Bridlington may be considered to date from 1818, the 670 feet long North Pier having been erected at that time. Nevertheless, there was a small landing place hereabouts long before that, a charter from King Stephen entitling the Priory to charge dues from ship owners who landed their vessels near the site of the present harbour, in the twelfth century.

The most famous person to come ashore at Bridlington in days gone by was Charles I's Queen, Henrietta Maria. She disembarked in 1643, after visiting Holland to enlist support for Charles I in return for some of the Crown Jewels. Aboard the ship were guns and ammunition, and Parliament sent four vessels to head her off and prevent her from landing.

They failed to do so, but cannonaded the town to such a degree that she fled to Boynton Hall, three miles inland, for refuge with Sir William Strickland, who was equally popular with both Roundheads and Royalists.

The Stricklands came to Boynton from Westmorland, and the founder of the Boynton branch of the family gave them their turkey crest as their coat-of-arms, because some such birds came into his possession while he was exploring the New World with Cabot.

In this way the popular Christmas dish was introduced into Britain, and the turkey still figures in the Strickland escutcheon, whilst the head of such a bird substitutes the customary eagle on the lectern in the village church.

Two miles more brings Rudston into view. Here lived Winifred Holtby, the novelist, and she lies in the churchyard. The most striking feature of the sacred precincts, however, is the monolith close to the church tower. Nearly 25 feet tall, the purpose is uncertain, and the method of erection is obscure. But it may mark the spot where primitive man worshipped, for the provision of a neverfailing spring, which is part of the Gipsy Race, an underground stream which emerges in the centre of Bridlington harbour and keeps that refuge and mooring place free from silt.

The most reliable explanation about the setting up of a monster column like this, without the use of lifting tackle, suggests that the full length exceeds 50 feet, and that it was found lying on the ground. A pit was then dug beneath more than half the length of the obelisk, causing it to tilt into an upright position.

Bridlington as a resort does not forget its illustrious personalities. In the public garden overlooking the harbour, and near Windsor Crescent, stands a sundial in memory of Lawrence of Arabia. He knew the locality well, having been stationed nearby while serving in the R.A.F. as Aircraftsman Shaw.

A further son of Bridlington was Humphrey Sandwith, born

there in 1822, who has a memorial fountain near the town hall. He organised hospitals in the Crimean War, and admitted wounded of British, Russian or Turkish nationality without discrimination. Later he turned successfully to writing popular books.

Neither does the resort forget the world's most famous airwoman, Amy Johnson, the one time office worker whose skill and daring brought her fame far beyond Yorkshire. Sewerby Hall, the Georgian mansion just outside Bridlington, has a room displaying many souvenirs of her epic flights.

North of Bridlington lies the formidable Flamborough Head, with the lighthouse, lifeboat station, sea-hewn caves, and sprawling village. Still farther in the same direction are the highest cliffs along the one hundred and seventeen miles between Spurn Point and the mouth of the Tees, together with the county's tiniest church, at Upleatham.

The tallest sea cliff, at Boulby, rises to 680 feet, and has long been an important meeting place for gulls and other seabirds, their future being assured by a ban on egg collectors, who in the past threatened the extinction of the colony. The claim of Upleatham Church to be the smallest in the county, or even in the whole country, fails when one realises that the structure is but a part of the edifice formerly on the site.

The 92 feet high Flamborough lighthouse was something of a builder's wonder when it was erected in 1806 by John Matson of Bridlington. He finished the job in only nine months and, incredibly, used no scaffolding.

The church at Flamborough has one of the only two surviving medieval rood lofts in Yorkshire, the other being at Hubberholme. The coastal sanctuary was the scene of a startling discovery in 1936 when the vicar found an old document in the church safe. It turned out to be a pardon granted by Charles II to Walter Strickland of Boynton, who was a signatory to the death warrant of Charles I.

The pardon had remained unsuspected in the church since the Restoration, having been kept there because Sir Walter was buried nearby in 1671.

The commanding site of Filey, on the same stretch of coastline, is a quieter resort than Scarborough, Bridlington, or Whitby. It attracted the Brontë sisters, but the only souvenir of the family preserved in the church is a carved bench-end in a case, this treasure being a survivor from the chancel stalls known to the visitors from Haworth.

The figure of a boy in the wall of the south aisle is often mistaken for Saint Oswald, the patron saint of Filey, whereas it is a representation of a 'boy bishop' whose rare custom was to keep order among the boys of the parish from 6th December to Christmas Eve. Another oddity is a cracked bell in the tower. It was damaged by too enthusiastic use when victories were celebrated by bellringing in the days of William Pitt.

South of Bridlington the line of the old coast road can be traced in the direction of Lissett, Ulrome, Skipsea, and Atwick to Hornsea. In Cardigan Road, Bridlington, is a milestone from the early traffic which followed this route.

Ulphus, the Saxon earl who gave his remarkably carved horn to York Minster, where it is preserved, is believed to have lived near Ulrome. An archaeological discovery in one of the nearby meadows in 1880 put the village in the news headlines. Excavators unearthed remnants of a 90 feet long wooden platform erected nearly twenty thousand years ago by men of the Stone Age whose homes were set on stilts driven into the bed of a lake that no longer exists.

Lake dwellers also founded Skipsea nine hundred years ago, where a mound shows the site of a castle built to protect their properties. The overlord was a mysterious Flemish adventurer called Drogo, husband of one of William the Conqueror's daughters. Drogo was given part of the Yorkshire Holderness for his services at the Battle of Hastings, but fled across the sea when he was sought for committing a crime.

The castle was demolished towards the end of the thirteenth century, and the mound is all that survives from it today. More tangible are four bare patches in a field close to the earthworks. Efforts to grow grass on the patches are said to be always unsuccessful because they mark the spot of a deadly duel fought by two Danish troopers in the seventeenth century.

The 'Cathedral of the Wolds' is a description applied to Bainton Church, six miles or so from Driffield, but the same distinction has been accorded to some East Riding shrines, notably Hedon Church, which is also known as the 'King of the Holderness'. Patrington Church is the 'Queen' of the region north-east of Hull.

As to Hornsea, few holidaymakers would associate the resort with a pitched battle by monks who sought to debar others from fishing in the Mere, Yorkshire's biggest lake. However, just such a conflict did occur when the fishing rights were claimed by the Abbot of Meaux Abbey, despite the fact that the same privilege had been granted to St. Mary's Abbey, York.

The holy friars had the issue fought out in a battle lasting a whole day, victory going to those from York. Then the winners generously agreed to the Meaux brethren catching fish from south side of the Mere.

Nowhere else in the East Riding is there a place to rival Beverley for history and antiquities both religious and secular. An introduction to this enchanting town is best made by approaching from the north and entering through the North Bar, a portal which once impressed itself on the design of local buses. The vehicles which pass through this gateway used to have their roofs specially shaped to negotiate the arch with just a few inches to spare, although now this is no longer necessary.

The Bar was, of course, part of the defences protecting Beverley Minster. The town walls were at one period punctuated by four other old gateways. The North Bar, the last to survive, had stood for four hundred and fifty years until it underwent restoration in the last century and was given new side entrances.

The Magnificent Minster is the only church in the country with bells which mark the hours in separate towers. This story began about the year 700, when the fifth Bishop of York, John of Beverley, established a monastery here. Forays by Danes, and fires subsequently put it out of use, and the Minster confronting us today dates from a rebuilding scheme started in 1220, but not finished until one hundred and eighty years later.

The structure incorporates materials obtained from the ruins of St. Mary's Abbey, York, and to this day it has a medieval treadmill used for lifting masonry to the roof for repair work. One of the most treasured possessions is the ancient frid stooll, or sanctuary chair, which gave refuge to pursued criminals, and ensured that they received a fair trial.

A competitor to the Minster is St. Mary's Church, with a beautiful exterior, and an extremely colourful interior. Lewis Carroll visited here whilst staying with some Beverley friends, and there is a sculpture of a dressed-up hare with a schoolboy's satchel slung from his shoulder. The parson-writer of *Alice's Adventures in Wonderland* may have modelled his March Hare after the carving.

A rare circumstance is that Beverley has three market days, and the area known as Saturday Market boasts one of the finest and most historic market crosses in the country. The structure is much more than a mere column, consisting of a cupolar'd roof over an octagonal open-sided erection with supporting pillars. On top of everything is a turret.

This market shelter was built in the early eighteenth century and was paid for by the town's two Members of Parliament. The town's arms appear on it, together with the royal arms of France and England.

Midway between Beverley and Hull is Cottingham, once describing itself as the biggest village in England. Nowadays, it is a dormitory for commuters to Hull, but the charm has not been marred. It used to have a castle, but this has disappeared, only the mound which supported it having survived. The fortress was built in 1170, and was known as Baynard Castle.

The strangest incident in its history was the occasion when it was deliberately burned down by Lord Wake in Tudor days. Although the Wake family had entertained or protected royalty in earlier times, including King John and Edward I, Lord Wake was loth to have Henry VIII as a guest. Henry's reputation was well known, and the earl did not wish his lovely wife to meet the monarch. So tinder was placed in and around the castle and set alight. It went up in flames, giving Lord Wake a valid reason for denying hospitality to Henry when the Royal court came to East Yorkshire.

The new face of Hull, achieved since the end of the Second World War by dealing with the areas irrevocably damaged or totally destroyed in air raid, is attractive with colourful public gardens. The pleasant Queen's Gardens, however, are not attributable to the repairing of wartime destruction. A convenient retreat for shoppers, they were created in prewar days by filling in Hull's oldest dock.

The port derived its official name, Kingston-upon-Hull, from a visit paid to the vicinity by Edward I. Sailing up the Humber, he was so delighted with the way the bankside villages of Myton and Wike blended together that he decreed the combined settlement should be called 'King's Town upon Hull'.

That occasion was in fact the origin of the seaport, and its growth was rapid. The wealth of the place in medieval days can be judged from the fact that in 1359 Hull contributed sixteen warships and four hundred and sixty-six men for Edward III's wars against the French. They represented the third largest seaport in the kingdom, a status that has continued to this day.

Continuous too is a Yorkshire event in the horseracing calendar, though it is unknown to many Turf enthusiasts. The Wolds have been the setting for an annual four-mile breakneck gallop along the 'roof' of the East Riding, and this contest is considered to be the oldest horserace in the country. Long before the Epsom and Ascot racecourses were founded, riders were racing their mounts competitively along the old Roman Road near Market Weighton.

The contest has been held regularly since 1519, and entrants spur their steeds through five parishes before reaching the winning post at Kiplingcotes Farm, close to Middleton-on-the-Wolds. The race takes place on the third Thursday in March, but there is no official starting time. The 'off', however, is usually between noon and one o'clock.

At one time members of noble families took part, and there was heavy betting on the result of the race. Even today the winner receives prize money prescribed by Lord Burlington in 1618. He and some other enthusiastic Yorkshire racegoers established a fund of £360, and the winner gets the interest from this sum. At one time the investment brought in about £14 but nowadays the amount seldom reaches £6.

Prize money is also provided by the entrants, each paying £4 stake money. This goes to the rider who comes in second, so in recent years the winner has often received less than the runner-up! The judge and clerk of the course must be the lowest paid turf officials in the country, their fee being 25p.

Of great antiquity among sporting contests, too, is the competition for the Scorton Arrow, an archery prize named after the North Riding hamlet near Richmond. The award is a silver arrow made in the reign of Queen Elizabeth I, and the first match took place in May 1673 on the local green.

Originally only archers residing in a fairly restricted area were eligible, but the scope of the contest has latterly been extended, over-ruling the seventeenth century regulation which states that the competition 'shall always be held within six miles of Eriholme-upon-Tees in the County of York'.

Nowadays the event takes place anywhere in the county, and the choice of venue is granted to the current holder of the Scorton

Arrow. The trophy goes to the first archer striking the inner gold
of the sailcloth target, but other awards and distinctions are also
available. Consequently the event starts at 11 a.m. and goes on for
four hours with an interval for lunch.

Prized possessions of the Society of Scorton Archers include the
record book of all the shoots in the long history of the club. Other
items associated with the occasion are a silver horn, used to signify
the opening of the contest, a silver cup, and an ancient horn spoon.

Americans have a special interest in Scorton, Kiplin Hall near
the village having been built by the first Lord Baltimore. His son
so admired the Pilgrim Fathers, that he collected three hundred
persecuted individuals and sailed with them to the New World in
1633, thus founding Maryland, with its now biggest city named
after him. When the second Lord Baltimore died during a return
visit to England, the colonisation of the new American state was
continued by *his* son.

In the shadow of the Wolds, but only seven miles inland from
Bridlington, is one of Yorkshire's oft-visited stately homes. The
Tudor gateway of Burton Agnes Hall can be seen from the road
to Driffield, and behind it the mansion shelters amidst trees.

The royal crest over the entrance reveals that the mansion was
built in Elizabeth's reign. In fact it superseded a Norman house,
and part of this manorial property has survived—a circumstance
almost unmatched in connection with the development of any other
great residence in the land. The Norman house at Burton Agnes is
of such historic importance that it has been scheduled as an Ancient
Monument.

The interior of the Tudor mansion is rich in furnishings, and
contains intricately carved features, such as an elaborately sculptured chimney-piece in the Great Hall, a piece of sixteenth century
craftsmanship with panels showing Biblical scenes by Italian artists.

Such a residence is naturally not lacking in legends, and one
spine-chilling story is centred round a skull regarded as the head
of a murdered maidservant. She was found just before she
died, and her last request was for her skull to be kept in the Hall.
When a later occupant of the mansion had the horrible relic thrown
away, frightening happenings ensued. Objects flew through the air
without any apparent agency, and other articles shattered without
any reasonable cause. These manifestations of illbodings did not
cease until the skull was retrieved and bricked up in its niche again.

CHAPTER X

Yorkshire Worthies and Eccentrics

Yorkshire has bred many illustrious personalities, from the Brontës, to Captain Cook, to John Carr, to John Smeaton, and Thomas Chippendale. Yorkshire has, however, many remarkable sons, less famous, none more inventive than John Harrison of Foulby.

Without the help of Harrison's horological genius, the exploration of the South Seas begun by Cook would have been sorely handicapped, for accurate timekeeping was, and still is, a vital part of navigation. Courses across the oceans are charted by using a precise timepiece, and observing the relative positions of heavenly bodies at specific moments.

John Harrison made sailing the seas an exact science by providing mariners with clocks capable of keeping time to the high degree necessary, enabling them to pinpoint their position even when out of sight of land.

His chronometer was the first sufficiently reliable to satisfy the high standard laid down by the British Government in 1714, when a reward was offered for a really accurate marine timekeeper.

Harrison was born at Foulby, near Wragby, five miles from Wakefield, in 1693, his father being a carpenter employed by Sir Rowland Winn at Nostell Priory. He was baptised at Wragby Church. which stands just inside the gateway to the Winn estate.

Though he was never educated well enough to express his ideas clearly in writing, John Harrison's scientific turn of mind soon became evident. Probably by reason of his father's trade, some of his earliest clocks were made largely of wood.

One of these, with wooden wheels and ratchets, is in the Science Museum, London, and is still in good working order. He constructed it in 1713, by which time he was living in Barrow-on-Humber.

One of Harrison's horological inventions at that period was a special type of pendulum which prevented clocks from losing or gaining when changes of temperature lengthened or shortened this part of the timepiece.

Known as a 'grid-iron' pendulum, it consisted of a series of parallel rods, alternately steel and brass. With this arrangement the downward expansion of the steel rods was exactly compensated by the upward expansion of the brass ones.

Harrison also fitted a secondary spring to keep his clocks going while being wound up, and he experimented with an improved escapement.

His interest in marine timekeepers was given a big fillip when he learned that the Government were prepared to pay £10,000 for a clock which would enable a vessel to reach the West Indies from Britain without straying more than one degree from the course.

The prize was increased to £20,000 if the timepiece did not err more than two minutes during the six weeks' voyage.

The Yorkshire born clockmaker determined to make an all-out attempt to win the award. He spent several years in trying out his ideas, and at last, in 1728, when he was thirty-five, he considered that he had designed a chronometer which would meet the stringent requirements.

So far, however, his clock existed only in the form of detailed drawings, and when he brought them to London he was advised to return to Barrow-on-Humber and build a working model. This he did, spending a further seven years on the task before showing the Government committee a timepiece which he claimed would meet all their needs.

It was a cumbersome piece of mechanism, spring-driven, with two balances oscillating in opposite directions to counteract the ship's movements. There was also a device to meet the effects of temperature changes on the balance springs—the first time such an arrangement had ever been fitted to a clock.

Preliminary tests were made with this advanced chronometer on a voyage to Lisbon, after it had been tried out on a Humber barge. These trials were so successful that Harrison was given an honorarium of £200 to continue his work.

Indeed, he made no fewer than four of these improved clocks before deciding that everything was ready for the trip to the West Indies. The crucial test began in 1761, when Harrison sailed for Jamaica aboard H.M.S. *Deptford*, taking his latest chronometer with him.

When the ship berthed at its destination the instrument had erred by only five seconds—a result so unexpected that the Government officials thought a fluke had occurred!

They withheld payment of the reward, pending the outcome of a second test. It took Harrison another three years to make such further arrangements, but on this occasion the clock did even better. It erred less than on the earlier voyage!

Even so, Harrison failed to get the full payment promised. He was paid only £5,000 at once, and had to appeal to George III before the balance was forthcoming in 1773.

By this time he was eighty years old, and he did not benefit much from his hard-earned fortune, for he died three years later.

However, thanks to his genius, skill, and persistence, mariners were henceforward able to have extremely accurate timekeepers to help them in navigating around the globe.

Even in death, Harrison was not acclaimed and was misrepresented. His tombstone at Hampstead, London, was not inscribed until long after his burial, and it is thought that the long interval is the reason why several of the details on the stone are wrong.

It makes a strange memorial for a Yorkshireman who, throughout his lifetime, was closely concerned with extreme accuracy.

The West Riding textile industry owes a perpetual debt to a Farsley-born parson, who sailed to Australia early last century as the chaplain for the convict settlement then being established in New South Wales. He preached the first Christmas Day sermon there to transported criminals, and exercised strict religious control in the colony, as well as serving in secular courts of justice. He espoused the well-being of the aborigines, and his improvement of their circumstances earned him their deep respect and admiration.

Yet the Reverend Samuel Marsden achieved his lasting fame in quiet a different category. In 1808, during an audience with George III, he wore a suit made of Australian wool from a small consignment sent by him for processing by a mill manager at Rawdon, near Leeds, and which had been stored at Farsley pending such use. The king was so interested that he gave the clergyman five Spanish sheep to take back with him to Australia, where he was a farmer as well as a missionary and magistrate.

From this small flock developed the vast sheep farms of Australia, and the importation into Britain of the wool needed for the textile industry.

YORKSHIRE WORTHIES AND ECCENTRICS   141

Farsley, where Samuel Marsden was born in 1764, does not forget him, though elsewhere his influence on the staple industry of the West Riding is less generally recognised. The cottage where he lived as a child has vanished, but his local admirers put a tablet on the site a few years ago, with a bronze medallion bearing his portrait, and an inscription describing his career.

An obelisk in the village churchyard gives further testimony to this Farsley worthy, and although the present church was not erected until 1843, it contains a memorial window to him.

'Prize Pugilist to Pit Magnate' would be an apt title for a biography of John Gully, whose resting place is in the parish churchyard at Ackworth, near Pontefract. Though no National Coal Board memorial to him has been built, or is ever likely to be erected, his career is inseparable from the story of West Riding coalmining. He invested large sums in the early expansion of the industry, and helped to finance the opening of several pits in the Pontefract and Wakefield areas in the early nineteenth century.

Yet this benefactor to Yorkshire was neither a native of the county nor an industrialist. His main claim to fame stems from his remarkable feats as a prize-fighter. Butcher, bankrupt, pugilist, racehorse owner, country squire—that sums up his astonishing life story.

Born in 1781 at Wick, a village between Bristol and Bath, Gully inherited his father's butchery business but failed to make it pay, and was jailed for his debts. He took his first step up the ladder of fame when he was persuaded to take part in an impromptu sparring match with Henry Pearce, the Champion Prizefighter of England, better known as the 'Game Chicken'.

Gully acquitted himself so well in the barefist encounter that the onlookers subscribed to pay his debts and obtained his release from prison. In consequence he fancied his prospects rosy enough to take on the champion in an official fight at Hailsham, Sussex.

The event attracted a huge crowd, including members of the aristocracy. Among them was the Duke of Clarence, the future William IV. The battle lasted sixty-four rounds, and although Gully was battered, bruised, and beaten, his tremendous courage was so much admired that he was regarded as the new Champion of England when Pearce retired from prize-fighting shortly afterwards.

The one-time bankrupt butcher, in fact, was not seriously challenged for another two years. When at length he was called upon to meet Bob Gregson, the 'Lancashire Giant', so many spectators collected that the military authorities thought the French had landed in England, and the Volunteers were called out!

Over a hundred noblemen in carriages and on horseback came to watch the fight, and the pugilists wore white breeches and silk stockings, but no shoes. The match was shorter than the one with the 'Game Chicken', Gully putting his opponent down for the count in the twenty-seventh round.

The big purse he received for this victory enabled him to retire from prize-fighting and become a racehorse owner. In this sphere again he was markedly successful. A half share in the winners of the Derby and the St. Leger in 1832 netted him £85,000 and enabled him to purchase the extensive Ackworth estate.